The Theater of Michel Vinaver

David Bradby

Ann Arbor

THE UNIVERSITY OF MICHIGAN PRESS

842
V76zb

Copyright © by the University of Michigan 1993
All rights reserved
Published in the United States of America by
The University of Michigan Press
Manufactured in the United States of America

1996   1995   1994   1993   4   3   2   1

A CIP catalogue record for this book is available from the British Library.

Library of Congress Cataloging-in-Publication Data

Bradby, David.
     The theater of Michel Vinaver / David Bradby.
          p.   cm. — (Theater—theory/text/performance)
     Includes bibliographical references and index.
     ISBN 0-472-10326-1
     1. Vinaver, Michel, 1927–   —Criticism and interpretation.
     I. Title.   II. Series.
     PQ2643.I523Z59   1993
     842'.914—dc20   93-2632
                                                          CIP

Acknowledgments

I should like to express my gratitude to Michel Vinaver for his generous help and encouragement and for permission to quote extensively from his writings on the theater. My thanks also go to the Camargo foundation in Cassis, where the first chapters of this book were drafted. An early version of parts of chapters 1 and 6, together with an abbreviated chronology, appeared in *New Theatre Quarterly* 27 (August 1991); I am grateful to the editors for permission to use that material here.

Contents

Chapter 1

Dramaturgical Principles

Michel Vinaver's career as a playwright stretches over four decades, during which time his work has always been in the forefront of dramaturgical experiment in France. His plays have been staged at all the major theaters—the Théâtre National Populaire (T.N.P.), Théâtre National de Strasbourg, Comédie Française, Odéon, among many others—and have been produced by leading directors such as Roger Planchon, Antoine Vitez, Jean-Marie Serreau, Charles Joris, Alain Françon, Jacques Lassalle. But he has not become identified with any one theater or dramatic movement, retaining his independence as an author from changing fashions in theater production. The nearest he has come to being part of a "school" was in the 1970s, when French critics began to use the term *Théâtre du Quotidien* (Theater of the Everyday) to designate a group of playwrights that included Vinaver, Deutsch, and Wenzel in France as well as Kroetz, Achternbusch, and others in Germany. In fact, Vinaver's work had been centered on the experience of the Everyday since the late 1940s. His first novel, published in 1950, was entitled *Lataume, ou la vie quotidienne* (Lataume, or everyday life), and his first play, written five years later, was in its first draft entitled simply *Aujourd'hui* (Today).

Vinaver has described his attitude toward the Everyday in the following terms:

My relationship with the Everyday is one going back unchanged to my infancy and which is at the very center of my creative work. I recall that, as a child, I was astonished when permitted to do the simplest things, such as open a door, run, stop running, etc. I was both astonished and enraptured at being given these rights; I was always afraid that they would be withdrawn and that I would be thrust back into nonexistence. In this way the everyday was something highly charged, on the brink of transgression, at all events precarious, undeserved. *(Ecrits sur le théâtre,* 123)[1]

Because he had a sense of standing somehow *outside* reality, creative writing became for him not an exercise in imitating reality but, rather, a constant attempt to capture or penetrate a domain never perceived as given in advance: "In other words for me, as a writer, nothing exists before I begin to write, and the activity of writing becomes an attempt to give consistency to the world and to myself within it"(123–24).[2]

This experience of the world, as something not given in advance but constituted in and through the act of writing, provides an essential key to understanding Vinaver's work. Almost obsessively, he insists upon the banality, the ordinariness, the absolute flatness of the material from which he begins. Many of his plays do indeed depict very ordinary situations: a tourist hotel *(Iphigénie Hôtel);* a pair of semidetached houses with a shared terrace *(Les Voisins);* a man thrown out of work *(La Demande d'emploi).* And yet there are others that contradict this, whose situations are the very opposite of ordinary: a French soldier befriended by Korean villagers during the war in Korea *(Les Coréens);* a teenager's involvement in drugs leading to his arrest *(Dissident, il va sans dire);* a medical student who kills her lover *(Portrait d'une femme).* The play with the most out-of-the-ordinary situation of all is the one entitled *L'Ordinaire,* which takes place on a mountainside high in the Andes, where a group of plane crash victims survives by turning to cannibalism. The relationship between the ordinary and the extraordinary in these plays is more one of creative tension than of contradiction, for Vinaver sees the work of the playwright as being to empty these situations of their melodramatic potential, to prevent the usual presuppositions and interpretative grids from falling easily into place, and to show how such events are lived through so that they become part of someone's ordinary, everyday experience.

This is what he means by saying that he starts from the Everyday: it is the material realities of lived experience that furnish the starting point, not an idea or a thesis. Vinaver is an obsessive reader and classifier of newspaper articles; the primary source for his writing is often a news item taken from a paper (the word for a newspaper in French is *quotidien*). Through the work of composition there emerges what he terms *une pousée vers le sens,* a thrust toward meaning. Under the heading *Construction* (i.e., structure or composition) he wrote:

> At the start of a play there is no meaning. But as soon as the play is begun there is a thrust toward meaning, a thrust toward the formation of situations, themes, characters. Beginning with a shapeless nucleus, the product of the initial explosion, the play constructs itself bit by bit. At the end, if it is a success, it will appear as rigorously structured as if there had been a preexisting plan. (*Ecrits sur le théâtre*, 130)[3]

Writing for Vinaver is thus a process of *composition*, not of *interpretation*. The result aims to surprise, stimulate, and question its readers/spectators; it will not preach to or attempt to convert them. The author does not start with didactic intentions, does not claim to know something he can then pass on through his writing. In fact, his intention in composing the play is to create a work that will to some extent resist interpretation, in the sense of not being easily expressed in different terms, not reducible to paraphrase or to a "message." This is what Antoine Vitez meant when he described *Iphigénie Hôtel* as "insoluble," meaning "something that cannot be dissolved."

Such terms are more often used of poets than of playwrights, which is entirely appropriate, since Vinaver's compositional method was learned from studying poetry, especially the poetry of T. S. Eliot. At the age of nineteen, when he was a student in the United States, he had discovered *The Waste Land,* a poem that was to exert a powerful influence over his whole life as a creative writer. Through it he first served an apprenticeship to literature, translating the poem into French in 1947, just before he began to write his first novel. Since then it has continued to haunt him: "I know now that my encounter with *The Waste Land* was the very foundation of my work as a playwright (which began in 1955). It was far more than an influence. For a long time I was unaware of how much *The Waste Land* lived in me. More precisely I live in it. It is my home" (*La Terre vague*, 4).[4] In his plays Vinaver was to recreate Eliot's rhythms, his counterpoint of all kinds of styles and linguistic idioms: echoes of Dante, for example, juxtaposed with the most banal conversations. Eliot himself summed up the difficulties of this approach:

> And so each venture
> Is a new beginning, a raid on the inarticulate
> With shabby equipment always deteriorating

> In the general mess of imprecision of feeling,
> Undisciplined squads of emotion.

(Collected Poems, 203)

Vinaver's plays remain true to the inarticulacy and imprecision of feeling that are part of everyday life. Like Eliot in the Prufrock poems and in *The Waste Land,* he presents us with the figures who make up the ordinary world of business and commerce. Like Eliot, too, he will often bring this everyday world into collision with mythical archetypes. He has spoken of the "mythic shuttle" that is non-Aristotelian, coming and going between different stories, different time scales, different historical periods, weaving a linguistic texture with multiple resonances and revealing points of articulation between experiences of different orders. The hero of his first novel felt himself to be "caught between two myths"; many of the characters in his plays share a sense of being trapped in ready-made responses to the world. Some manage to escape; some do not.

Vinaver's compositional method results in plays that are not to be judged by the Aristotelian criteria traditional in France. Eugène Vinaver (the uncle of Michel) once suggested that, in the Aristotelian perspective, plays might be judged by how easily they submit to paraphrase. The most perfect example would be *Bérénice,* reduced by Racine himself to the six-word phrase of Suetonius, "Titus, reginam Berenicen dimisit invitus invitam." In contrast to this, he pointed out, "no summary, no paraphrase can do justice to *The Waste Land* any more than to *The Song of Roland* or *Beowulf,* or *Piers Plowman.*" In these works he detected a different kind of integrity, "not the integrity of a pivotal centre, narrative or conceptual, but that of a close-knit fabric, the various strands of which are inseparable from one another, and yet not subordinate to any single one of them" ("Medieval Poetry and the Moderns"). This describes exactly the integrity of Vinaver's plays. They proceed by the interweaving of many different strands in such a way that no one dominates but all are inseparable. This produces a polyvalent drama well characterized by a comparison with the cubist art of Braque or Picasso: in these plays the traditional perspective, which relies on a single, stable viewpoint, is overturned in favor of multiple viewpoints, discontinuities, and contradictions. Like cubist painting, like the poetry of Eliot or the prose of Joyce, Vinaver's fragmented, multiple viewpoint is both statement and formal device. It states the impossibility of ever returning to a completely unified, coherent worldview and asserts that only meanings, not meaning, can be found.

To understand the full originality of Vinaver's approach to play writing it is necessary to place his work in the context of other experimental theater work in the 1950s. Modern French experimental theater traces its origin back to the first performance of *Ubu Roi* by Alfred Jarry in 1896. This play was designed by its creator to be an insult thrown in the face of all cultured Parisian theatergoers. It deliberately undermined every expectation of its audience: it was utterly unrealistic in opposition to the triumphant naturalism of Antoine; it was crude and brash, though performed in a theater known for the delicate nuances and atmospheric half-tones of symbolism; it was antiheroic at a time when almost nobody questioned the need for heroes; it was antihistorical at a time when historical verisimilitude was the mark of much innovative staging. The offense was understood by the first-night audience: the play was buried by common consent. Jarry died young in 1907 but was admired by the Surrealists who succeeded in having his reputation reinstated as an innovator to be taken seriously. When Antonin Artaud attempted to found his first theater company in 1926 he named it after Alfred Jarry. Nevertheless, Jarry remained a little-known cult figure until the mid-1950s when, in the wake of the success of the "New" theater of Beckett, Ionesco, Adamov, Genet, etc., people began to search for the antecedents of this new art of cruelty and absurdity. They discovered them in Artaud, in the Surrealist theater, and in Jarry.

The mid-1950s was also the period in which Vinaver was becoming involved for the first time in theater work. The circumstances were the result of his taking a job with Gillette, then setting up its French offices in Annecy. Casting around for cultural events in Annecy, Vinaver took an interest in a summer festival for theater students and amateurs run by Gabriel Monnet (later to become the first director of the first Maison de la Culture at Bourges). Vinaver was invited by Roland Barthes (a friend since 1947) to contribute an article about Monnet's production of *Hamlet* for the recently founded review *Théâtre Populaire*. This article records his excitement in discovering "that theater does not demonstrate a point, but lays out the facts. It is not a proposition but a revelation" (*Ecrits sur le théâtre,* 25).[5] The following summer Vinaver took an active part in the work of the theater festival, organizing a session on the origins of Greek theater in initiation rites and presenting a montage of interwoven stories drawn from James Thurber and from Chinese folklore. To follow *Hamlet* Monnet had chosen *Ubu Roi;* the sulphurous quality still retained by Jarry's work in 1955 can be seen by the fact that the municipal authorities

threatened a veto. The production could only go ahead after the support
of Jean Vilar, Albert Camus, Jean Dasté, and other luminaries (including
Barthes and Vinaver himself) had been canvased.

Writing about *Ubu Roi* that summer, Vinaver identified the principal
elements of what was to become his own play-writing practice. In the
first place he noted that the theater has always possessed an aggressive
charge, and the aggressive force of *Ubu* lay in its assault on habitual ways
of thinking and received ideas (*Ecrits sur le théâtre*, 35). Second, he
saluted Jarry's attack on well-made plays of character study, an attack
that was to be developed much more profoundly by Artaud between the
wars and was to find its fulfillment in the New theater: *"Ubu Roi* makes a
splendid *tabula rasa* of chronological continuity, psychological continuity, even the logical continuity of dramatic action" (32).[6] Third, Vinaver
insisted on the *innocence* of Ubu, likening him to the figure of Charlie
Chaplin (known in France by the affectionate diminutive Charlot). In the
form of a puppet or cartoon character Ubu represented for Vinaver the
terrible innocence of the child who has not yet learned to repress his basic
drives. He emphasized the vigorous, inventive quality of the play and
insisted (as Peter Brook was to do twenty years later in his *Ubu aux
Bouffes*) on the roots of the play's appeal in the popular clowning tradition. What he most admired was the apparently haphazard structure, "following a movement that reinvents itself with each successive moment"
(32).[7]

Through the work on *Ubu Roi* Vinaver was led to reflect on more
general problems of dramaturgy and to make the link with the ancient
Greek history that he had studied at Wesleyan University. For a writer
growing up in France in the 1930s and 1940s it would have been quite
natural to turn to the Greek myths; versions of these myths by writers such
as Cocteau, Giraudoux, Anouilh, and Sartre had been the mainstay of
serious theater for the previous three decades. But Vinaver's education
had been different. He knew little of the French theater of the period, and
his Greek studies had been anthropological rather than dramaturgical,
American rather than French. He rejected the easy exploitation of allegori-
cal parallels between myth and modern reality as typified in Anouilh's
Antigone. The importance of Greek myth for the modern theater was not,
in Vinaver's view, that it provided a convenient source of stories but,
rather, in what it taught about the function of theater: that of moving
people from one state to another, from one point of view to another, from
one attitude to another. "It is not without interest," he wrote in 1956, in

a program note to his first play, "that the origin of Greek theatre is to be found in initiation rites through which, in tribal societies, the passage is made from childhood to manhood, from winter to spring, *from one situation to another*" (*Ecrits sur le théâtre,* 154).[8] Like Artaud, he identified the function of theater as fundamentally aggressive, though he did not, like Artaud, devalue language in favor of mise-en-scène; he considered that Artaud had made a mistake in identifying the written dramatic text with the stultifying "discussion plays" of his day. He insisted that a successful play text is an autonomous work, lending itself equally well to private reading or to public staging.

During the 1950s, for the first time, the presence of Artaud and Brecht began to be felt as the two major but contradictory influences on French theater. Vinaver learned from both but was not willing to accept enrollment in either camp. He was wary of Artaud's insistence that the director should become the sole creative force on the modern stage. In a world that had lost contact with the dimension of the sacred he felt that Artaud's yearning for total theater on the Balinese model was utopian. Artaud's vision implied a transformation of every aspect of life; there was an obvious danger of this ideal leading to very superficial results if confined to the theater profession alone.

Brecht, who was the other major influence on French theater, seemed closer to Vinaver's concerns, since the young French author had been introduced to the theater by Gabriel Monnet, Roland Barthes, Bernard Dort, and the editorial team of *Théâtre Populaire*. From them he acquired a vision of theater as a vital, public art form, engaged with the struggles of its day and accessible to all. Together with this vision went a serious reflection on the function of theater within the community and an unusual openness to new forms of dramatic construction. It was in the pages of *Théâtre Populaire* that the Brechtian Epic theater was most vigorously (as well as most sympathetically) analyzed and its implications spelled out for new French play writing. For Vinaver's own work the most important element of the new Epic dramaturgy was its rejection of the Aristotelian unities—not only this, but also the fact that Brecht went out of his way to exploit interruptions, discontinuities, and contradictions in his development of story and presentation of character.

One of the main features of Brecht's work to be analyzed by the *Théâtre Populaire* team was its demystification of familiar ideological constructs; indeed, Barthes went on to do something similar, in nondramatic form, with his *Mythologies*. When *Les Coréens* was staged, with its demystification of wars of "liberation," Vinaver was hailed as "the French Brecht." But it soon became clear that ideological demystification was not his central concern. Barthes himself saw this very clearly, commenting that: "the novelty of the work is, paradoxically, to be situated, as it were, in pre-ideological territory, without this ever becoming a solution of irresponsibility" (*Théâtre I*, 37). Although Vinaver evolved a dramatic method having something in common with Brecht's in its epic, discontinuous form, it did not share the didactic charge that is present, to a greater or lesser extent, in all Brecht's work. As Barthes commented, the *gestus* is different. Social and political relations *are* demonstrated, but not in order to demystify or to clarify a set of contradictions; they seem, rather, to open up the possibility of a theater of reconciliation only glimpsed, in Brecht's work, in the prologue to *The Caucasian Chalk Circle* (40).

By the late 1950s Vinaver had reached the point where, while placing the highest value on Brecht's work, he was alarmed by the growing tendency among some critics and theater people to be satisfied with simplistic interpretations of Brechtian theory. If distortions were to be avoided, Vinaver felt that there was a pressing need to place Brecht's work accurately in relation to other theater forms of the twentieth century. On a visit to New York in May 1958 he attended three working sessions of the Actor's Studio, directed by Lee Strasberg, and published an account of these visits, together with a meditation on Brecht and Stanislavsky in *Théâtre Populaire*. Here he expressed the view, uncommon in 1958, that "it would be the most enormous misunderstanding to imagine that Brecht substitutes reflection for emotion" (*Ecrits sur le théâtre*, 75).[9] No work of art can dispense with emotion: it has to affect the whole person, not just the mind, and Brecht's plays certainly have their effect on the spectator's emotions. Brecht, he agreed, had introduced a "new usage" into the theater, but his fundamental aim was no different from that of the Western theater tradition from Aeschylus to Stanislavsky: "to change men, to liberate them from the present that encloses them and to open up a new field of vision and of action" (75).[10] He pointed out that, if the *Verfremdungseffekten* are treated as an end in themselves, they lose their purpose, which is to introduce a "continual come-and-go between direct action and critical reflection, between participation and distancing, since the latter can only grow out of the former" (74).[11] Vinaver underlines here how his own reliance on a method of "come-and-go" operates as a Brechtian alienation effect.

To those who objected that Vinaver should have come out with a more clearly formulated political commitment he had already made reply through one of the characters in his novel *L'Objecteur*, who argues that the very idea of commitment is a "gigantic joke, since knowledge necessarily involves commitment" (*L'Objecteur*, 69). The act of writing is thus inevitably a commitment, since through it the writer gives consistency to the world. Yet it is not commitment in the sense of demonstrating a political thesis, since the act of writing starts from nothing: everything is to be discovered or revealed; nothing is to be proved. Albert Camus, who recommended the publication of both novels to Gallimard, commented that Vinaver's commitment was of a different kind: "Vinaver. The writer is ultimately responsible for everything he does. But he has to be willing . . . to remain in ignorance *while he is writing* of the conditions of that responsibility—to take a risk" (*Carnets: Janvier 1942–Mars 1951*, 266).[12]

In 1953 Vinaver, reflecting on Henry Green's *Loving*, which he had just translated, wrote something similar: "It is sufficient for the creator to apply himself to his work, to avoid being distracted by what he wants to say, to dare to commit himself (or abandon himself) completely to his material" (*Ecrits sur le théâtre*, 12).[13] The nature of this material, as Vinaver conceives of it, is in the first place linguistic. He is fond of describing language as his "raw material." The playwright's job is to assemble and shape the building blocks of language in such a way as to reveal how we construct our images of the world. It is very comparable to the aim Barthes set himself in his *Mythologies* (1957). In one of the essays of *Mythologies* Barthes wrote that Arthur Adamov's play *Le Ping-Pong* was "entirely composed of a block of frozen language not unlike those frozen vegetables which allow the English to enjoy in the middle of winter the fresh tastes of spring" (100). The strength of the electric pin table in Adamov's play was that it did not symbolize any one thing but acted as an irreducible object, giving rise to what Barthes called linguistic situations *(des situations de langage)*. Something of the same can be said of Vinaver's plays, in which the objects, myths, or themes engender a conflict at the linguistic level, although the blocks of language in Vinaver's plays constantly melt and refreeze. Close examination of the plays will show how different linguistic idioms confront one another, shift, break up, and re-form, with varying degrees of appropriateness to the characters who speak or the situations in which they find themselves. Jean-Pierre Sarrazac has pointed out that Vinaver does not present characters who, like Ionesco's, labor vainly under the weight of a dead or reified language (*L'Avenir du drame,* 115). On the contrary, his starting point is a rich and varied idiom, whose very variety gives it an a priori shapelessness but from which meanings will emerge through counterpoint, interruption, ellipsis, etc.

The method is the juxtapositional one learned from T. S. Eliot, and Vinaver's term to express it is *la mise en relation* (bringing into relationship or contact). He has written that these juxtapositions, or *mises en relation,* are "material in nature—that is to say they take place at the level of the linguistic material—rhythmic effects, collisions of sounds, shifts of meaning from one sentence to another" (*Ecrits sur le théâtre,* 125).[14] In order to dramatize this belief in language as raw material Vinaver has recourse to comparison with nonpropositional art forms, music and painting: "I work with words like a painter works with line and color or a musician with sound" (315).[15] Such comparisons are easily misunderstood; the meaning attached to them by Vinaver is different from the theater of abstract rhythms advocated by Ionesco, in which rhythm is everything and words are gradually emptied of meaning. On the contrary, words and rhythm combine in Vinaver's plays to engender "impulses toward meaning." Just as the pictures of Rauschenberg, for example, juxtapose images of different kinds, playfully allowing for the happy coincidence or the surprise of the unexpected, so Vinaver juxtaposes different linguistic registers, from high culture to low, from learned to familiar, from mythical to modern. In the texture of the completed dramatic dialogue they do not lose their quality of difference but acquire new resonances by virtue of those things with which they are brought into contact.

In drama character is always presented through a process of interaction. Vinaver's approach leads him naturally to exploit this as a strength: the characters in his plays are all defined by their relationships with one another. Just as Braque claimed that the important thing in his paintings was not so much the objects depicted as the space between them (see page 24), so Vinaver's characters can be seized only in the actions that take place between them. Each of his plays affords a wealth of insight into how "character" is composed of a constantly shifting network of interactions: between persons, between groups, between the individual and the group. There is practically no monologue in Vinaver's theater; speech is always part of a process of action and reaction with others. The multiplicity of voices that drama inevitably entails is fundamentally congenial to him. He welcomes the fact that the playwright, unlike other writers, cannot speak with his own voice but, instead, speaks only through the orchestration of other voices: "Dramatic writing suits me because in it I make others speak and because its language does not describe, nor comment, nor explain, but acts" (*Mémoire sur mes travaux*, 38).[16] This makes for plays in which conflict of character is always an important element.

A similar conflict, or tension, characterizes Vinaver's use of dramatic situation. Every one of his plays exploits a tension between the expectations of the characters and the situations in which they are placed. This is obvious enough in a play such as *L'Ordinaire*, whose characters are stranded on a mountain range; it is no less true of *La Demande d'emploi*, whose characters are stranded on the reef of unemployment. But, although Vinaver's characters find themselves in situations that impose restrictions, they are also allowed some freedom of maneuver; they face the need for change. The fragmented structures, which superimpose different stories, can provoke cracks in the established order, present the world in an unexpected light, suggest possibilities for a transition "from one situation to another." Although all Vinaver's plays present moments of profound emotion, the mood they most frequently create is one of ironic humor—humor sparked by the discrepancy between what is expected and what happens, the aspirations of the characters and the realities of their situations.

Vinaver's achievement lies in having abandoned a theater of linear narrative for one of multiple possibilities. In 1964 Armand Gatti invoked the need for different, parallel realities to be shown simultaneously on stage (*Chant public devant deux chaises électriques*, 15). Vinaver's plays represent a further refinement of similar ideas: he suggests that, if it is impossible to make sense of our lives as linear sequences, then we must go back to each separate situation and try out their possible combinations. In this way a new form of Epic theater is created, opposed to the Aristotelian like Brecht's, and depending on multiple viewpoint. Through the development of an original, polyvalent dramatic form, Vinaver has been able to explore the ways in which human beings adapt to the shifting realities of twentieth-century life. His is the first authentically Modernist theater, succeeding in "transforming the most uninteresting raw material into an object of enjoyment and knowledge" (*Ecrits sur le théâtre*, 132).[17]

NOTES

1. A l'égard du quotidien, j'ai un rapport ancien, un rapport enfantin. Un rapport qui remonte à l'enfance et qui n'a pas changé, et qui est au centre même de mon activité d'écrivain. Je crois bien qu'enfant, j'étais étonné qu'on me permette les choses les plus simples, comme de pousser une porte, de courir, de m'arrêter de courir, etc. . . . J'étais étonné, émerveillé de ces droits qu'on me donnait, et j'étais toujours à craindre qu'on me les retire, qu'on me repousse dans la non-existence. De la sorte, le quotidien, c'était quelque chose de très vibrant, au bord de l'interdit, en tout cas précaire, immérité.

2. Autant dire que pour l'écrivain que je suis rien n'existe avant d'écrire, et qu'écrire c'est essayer de donner consistance au monde, et à moi dedans.

3. Au départ d'une pièce il n'y a aucun sens. Mais aussitôt l'écriture de la pièce commencée, il y a une poussée vers le sens, une poussée vers la constitution de situations, de thèmes, de personnages. A partir d'un noyau indéterminé issu de l'explosion initiale, la pièce n'arrête pas de se construire. A la fin, si elle est réussie, elle se présente comme un objet aussi rigoureusement construit que s'il y avait un plan préalable.

4. En tant qu'ecrivain de théâtre (ce que j'ai commencé à être en 55) la rencontre avec *The waste land* a été, je le sais aujourd'hui, fondatrice. Beaucoup plus qu'une influence. Longtemps je suis resté sans avoir conscience que *The waste land* m'habitait. Plus exactement, je l'habite. C'est ma maison.

5. Le théâtre n'est pas une démonstration, il est une évidence. Il ne propose pas, mais révèle.

6. *Ubu-Roi,* superbement, fait table rase de la continuité chronologique, psychologique et simplement logique de l'action.

7. Suivant un mouvement qui s'invente d'instant en instant.

8. Il n'est pas indifférent que le théâtre grec ait eu pour origine les rites d'initiation au moyen desquels, dans les sociétés tribales, le passage se faisait de l'enfance à l'age de l'homme, de l'hiver au printemps, *d'une situation à une autre.*

9. Le plus grand contresens serait de supposer que Brecht substitute la réflexion à l'émotion.

10. De changer les hommes, de les libérer du présent qui les enferme, de leur ouvrir un champ neuf de vision et d'action.

11. Un "va-et-vient" continuel entre l'action directe et la critique, entre la participation et le distancement, celui-ci ne pouvant s'opérer qu'à partir de celle-là.

12. Vinaver. L'Ecrivain est finalement responsable de ce qu'il fait envers la société. Mais il lui faut accepter (et c'est là qu'il doit se montrer très modeste, très peu exigeant), de ne pas connaître d'avance sa responsabilité, d'ignorer, *tant qu'il écrit,* les conditions de son engagement—de prendre un risque.

13. Il suffit au créateur de s'appliquer à son travail, de ne pas se laisser distraire par ce qu'il a envie de dire, d'oser s'engager à fond dans la matière.

14. Je dirai un mot de ces mises en relation, de ces liaisons. Elles sont de nature *matérielle*—je veux dire, c'est au niveau de la matière du langage qu'elles se produisent—effets rythmiques, frottements de sons, dérapages de sens d'une phrase à une autre.

15. Je travaille la parole comme un peintre le trait et la couleur, comme un musicien le son.

16. L'Écriture théâtrale me va parce que ce sont d'autres que moi qu'elle fait parler, et parce que cette parole ne décrit pas, ne commente pas, n'explique pas, mais agit.

17. [Il faut que l'alchimie opère] qui transmute le magma le plus extrêmement inintéressant en un objet de jouissance et de connaissance.

Chapter 2

The First Decade

The four plays that Vinaver wrote in the 1950s were unique in the French theater of their time. In the dying years of the Fourth Republic no other dramatist was producing work based on the colonial wars in which France was then entangled, or on the ins and outs of political intrigue as each new government that was formed succumbed to a kind of exhaustion, only to reform with the same politicians slightly rearranged. Even more original than the subject matter was the method adopted by Vinaver, sticking close to the lived reality of his very ordinary participants, treating the great events of his day in paradoxically decentered fashion, so that hierarchical distinctions between important and unimportant people were questioned, upset, treated differently. The challenge that Vinaver set himself in these plays was to write without the benefit of hindsight, to open up a communication between stage and audience that would be immediate (in the sense of being unmediated by allegory, myth, or other imposed hierarchies of meaning).

In arriving at this aim Vinaver had been influenced by two things. One was his own experience of theater at work under Gabriel Monnet, when he had felt for himself the excitement when an audience is in sympathy with the action portrayed on stage, when the play "comes across" (and, conversely, the deadness when it does not). The other influence at work came through his friends on the *Théâtre Populaire* editorial committee, whose analyses of the role that the theater should play in the community made reference to Greek and Elizabethan models: the theater should once again become the space in which the significant public events of the day found expression. But he also remained true to his own sense of the everyday, turning his back on the grand heroic manner of Shakespeare or Corneille. With the partial exception of *Les Huissiers,* the action of all

Vinaver's plays and adaptations of this period represent the lives of ordinary people, lacking in political influence or historical importance. By sticking closely to contemporary reality, Vinaver achieved a quality similar to that found in Chekhov's plays: far from being uninteresting because they are not at the center of great events, the characters acquire general significance, become representative of anyone who has known the feeling of not being in control of his or her own fate, of having to maneuver within a range of strictly limited freedoms.

The characters of his first play, *Les Coréens,* exemplify this. The play presents its audience with an insignificant patrol of French soldiers (part of the United Nations [UN] expeditionary force) who have lost their way in the Korean bush and a group of equally insignificant villagers, one of many small farming communities that have had the misfortune to be caught between the opposing armies and partially destroyed. For a while it seems that this village may, after all, be singled out for distinction, as the northern army has sent word that it will pause for rest and food there as it pursues its progress toward the south. In the event the southerners fall back more quickly than expected, and the northern army presses on, bypassing the village altogether. So neither the French soldiers nor the Korean villagers are in a position to have any effect on the progress of the war.

In their relationships with one another, however, they demonstrate the whole range of reactions to it, by both Koreans and Westerners. Vinaver is able to introduce an enormous breadth of response, from hatred and scorn through the whole gamut of attitudes to love and reconciliation. The worlds of both French soldiers and Korean villagers are presented economically by means of dialogue characterized by an unusual mixture of familiar and unfamiliar elements: it abounds in clichés, and yet the clichés do not always imprison the speakers. They appear, for much of the time, to be conditioned by their language imposing its own structures on them, as in scene 3, where the soldiers play out an imaginary ceremony for the unveiling of a war memorial. But these linguistic impositions are not monolithic; they are fissured with hesitations, pauses, and contradictory impulses. The audience is constantly surprised by the intervention of a quite different language that breaks in on and questions the situation. So, for example, in the first scene between the Korean girl Wen Ta and the wounded French soldier Belair, they pass from talk of gun wounds to oranges. Belair's loving description of the sensation of peeling an orange becomes a shared link between them. In the course of the action Belair and some of the villagers (Wen Ta, Wou Long, and Lin Huai) find their responses to one another changing, as the propaganda clichés of wartime fail to fit the human reality they discover in one another. Other characters travel in the opposite direction, relating to one another in progressively more instrumental or exploitative fashion.

Les Coréens was written for Gabriel Monnet in the course of a few weeks in autumn 1955. At this time, however, Monnet had no permanent theater; the plan was to use Vinaver's play for next summer's theater festival. In the meantime Vinaver was eager for it to be performed. On a business visit to Lyon he attended a performance by Roger Planchon's company of *The Good Woman of Setzuan* and was so impressed by its quality that he offered his new play to Planchon, who accepted it immediately. *Les Coréens* was produced at the Théâtre de la Comédie in Lyon on 24 October 1956. Planchon's theater was unusual for its time, being the only fixed professional company then operating outside Paris, apart from the state-subsidized Centres Dramatique Nationaux. The latter were theater companies committed to an ideal of theater for the people and to touring around the area in which they were based. Their repertoires consisted mainly of Molière, Shakespeare, and other classics of the European tradition, presented in a spirit of cultural evangelism and designed to attract audiences with no previous habit of theatergoing. In this perspective new authors were considered to be too "difficult" and very rarely found their way into the repertoire. Planchon, on the other hand, was a twenty-five-year-old enthusiast determined to present the work of new authors and to establish himself in the vanguard of dramatic developments. At the time when he produced *Les Coréens* he was coming to terms with his recent discovery of Brecht. Both the plays and the theory of the German dramatist had hit him with the force of a revelation, provoking him to declare his intention to work as an apprentice to the master. It would not have been surprising, therefore, if his production had been excessively "Brechtian," emphasizing the anticolonial aspects of Vinaver's play. In fact, it seems that Planchon's sensitivity to concrete detail in production served the play extremely well.

Les Coréens was performed on a stage covered in earth, in which were planted clumps of reed. The difficult conditions for the soldiers, crawling through the brush on their bellies, trying to ambush an elusive enemy, were well conveyed by this setting. So also were the spartan conditions of village life in which the Koreans were trying to rebuild their bombed homes. It satisfied the two principal requirements of setting in

Vinaver's theater: on the one hand it provided a neutral space, a space that would only begin to take on connotations once it was occupied by people, whose words and actions would give it meaning. On the other hand it satisfied the need for physical materiality or plasticity: though never requiring detailed naturalistic settings, Vinaver's plays nevertheless emphasize the physical realities within which people live and move. As in Brecht's plays, objects and materials must be authentic, though they may be fragmentary or incomplete.

In 1956 the Korean War had been settled for three years, but France had recently suffered a terrible blow to national pride with the capture of its military base at Dien Bien Phu in Vietnam (May 1954) and its consequent withdrawal from Southeast Asia. Moreover, French forces were becoming ever more deeply committed in the war in Algeria. Right-wing elements supporting a strong French military presence abroad took Vinaver's play to be a provocation and stirred up riots outside the theater. These were serious at times and were accompanied by threats to the theater company. As a result of this agitation, the play attained instant notoriety, and Vinaver acquired a misleading reputation as a committed playwright. The Parisian critics all came to see the play, and their reviews were mostly favorable. It was a dazzling and, no doubt, heady debut for a young playwright. More important, from Vinaver's point of view, was the fact that the play had a second production by Jean-Marie Serreau in Paris later in the same season. (As well as Serreau's production, in January 1957, the play was also put on by Charles Joris in 1959 and by Gabriel Monnet in 1960.) Serreau's version was very different from Planchon's, relying less on physical representation, contenting itself with detailed attention to the rhythms of the text. The design, the first by André Acquart, created a neutral space, consisting of piles of stones on a bare stage. Vinaver felt that, though each of these productions had its faults, they succeeded, between them, in giving a satisfyingly complete scenic realization of the potentialities contained in the text. The experience of seeing his work performed had a stimulating effect: he wrote two and a half more plays in the period 1957–59.

The "half" consisted of chorus passages for *Antigone*. This came about as a result of official censorship: Monnet had intended to use *Les Coréens* for the summer festival of 1957, but the hostile propaganda that had been stirred up in response to Planchon's production led to an official veto by the Directeur Général de la Jeunesse et des Sports at the Ministry of Education, which funded the course. A letter from the director general made it clear that the play was not acceptable to an organization whose purpose was the promotion of great works of French dramatic literature ("de promouvoir les grandes oeuvres de notre littérature dramatique française") (*Mémoire sur mes travaux,* 53). Monnet was obliged to find another play, and so, with the idea of protest against officialdom in mind, he asked Vinaver to write a new version of *Antigone.* Vinaver decided not to do this but to use Paul Mazon's French translation of Sophocles' text instead, writing a new version of the chorus passages only. Performances were given in the costumes that had been prepared for *Les Coréens,* thus contributing to the protest against the ministerial censorship and underlining the antiauthoritarian message contained within the original play.

Vinaver's chorus passages are very remarkable. They mark the rediscovery of a genuine choral voice in the modern theater, solving at one stroke the problems that had defeated Giraudoux, Anouilh, and Eliot. Poetic choral writing always seems awkward on the modern stage: this form, predicated on a disciplined and "hierarchized" society, appears artificial in an age when social discipline and hierarchies are under attack. But Vinaver was able to show that there *is* an authentic twentieth-century choral voice, one that he found not in Eliot's plays but in *The Waste Land* or *Sweeney Agonistes:* it is the voice of many people speaking, but speaking in dissonance and discontinuity, at cross-purpose and in confusion. Far from resolving the inevitable contradictions in an audience's response to Antigone's actions, Vinaver's chorus passages preserve these contradictions, hesitations, and uncertainties, presenting a chorus of intermediaries between audience and action whose members are in a constant state of flux and turmoil.

This reclaiming of a specifically modern choral voice was to have great significance for all Vinaver's subsequent dramatic work, as emerged immediately in *Les Huissiers,* the play that he wrote between August and November 1957. It was an attempt to write a dramatic action molded closely on contemporary reality, benefiting from no hindsight or distance at all and which would give its audience a sense of being in direct contact with the world of politics. The most successful passages of the play are those in which the ushers speak. Their speeches are not attributed to named characters but set out like the voices in the chorus passages for *Antigone.* Their various statements preserve a variety of different attitudes toward the events on which they comment, yet they have no purchase on the events of the play. The ushers can only react and comment, like the chorus of an ancient Greek play. Their one strength is that they survive.

Ministers may come, and ministers may go, but the ushers have a certain permanence, and this awareness gives them a faintly detached attitude. Their interventions are amusing, surprising, unexpected, yet possessing the ring of truth.

The politicians whom they guide along the corridors of power are less successful as dramatic creations. Paradoxically, this is because they are *too* well rounded, too close to the traditional character study. They behave as if they belonged to a play by Salacrou in which the action dealt with the conflict between personal ambition and the realities of political power. And yet the thrust of the play as a whole is to suggest that, ultimately, these politicians are interchangeable. The playwright is thus caught in an uncomfortable contradiction: on the one hand he has to make the audience care about whether Paidoux will recover his political authority and personal prestige; on the other he has to show that, ultimately, it makes no difference. In *Les Coréens* there was no plot of this kind; there were several stories, none forming a center of interest in its own right but whose fascination lay in the manner of their interweaving. In *Les Huissiers* there is too much plot, or, rather, it is too unified. The action becomes separated out into central and marginal characters (politicians and ushers, respectively); only the marginal characters fit the dramaturgical structure, and so only they retain the audience's interest. The paradox of Vinaver's plays is that they succeed best when *all* the characters are marginal.

The atmosphere, both political and theatrical, of 1957–58 made it hazardous for Planchon to mount this play, as he had planned. With the Algerian war plunging toward crisis point, people were driven to take sides. As revelations of atrocities multiplied, the government became nervous, resorting to frequent censorship. In 1957 Planchon's production of *Paolo Paoli* by Adamov had proved such a success with the critics that he had been invited to bring it to Paris. It was seen at the Vieux Colombier Theater in January 1958, but its run was cut short because it was considered dangerously subversive by certain government officials. Vinaver had already been banned once, and Planchon, who had recently taken on the lease of the large municipal theater of Villeurbanne, a far cry from the small experimental Théâtre de la Comédie in which he had performed *Les Coréens,* felt he could not take further risks. Moreover, his conception of theater at this time was under the influence of Brecht and Marxist thought, which laid stress on the need for critical and historical distance in representational art. A play that deliberately avoided such distance, while also scrupulously avoiding a political "message," seemed quite inappropriate to the hectic circumstances. By May 1958 Charles de Gaulle had taken power, and the situation had changed so radically that this attempt to write "in direct contact" with reality was invalidated: the play became historical. Its main interest now is precisely as a historical document, especially since the publication in 1981 of *Le Livre des Huissiers,* which includes a mass of contemporary press cuttings and photographs as well as the text of the play itself.

In 1958, although *Les Huissiers* was not performed, Vinaver still felt closely involved with contemporary theater work because Jean Vilar commissioned him to make an adaptation of *The Shoemaker's Holiday* by Thomas Dekker for the Théâtre National Populaire. Work on this play took Vinaver one stage further in defining the particular direction of his own dramaturgical experiments. Dekker's play is a friendly, domestic piece, written around 1600, which follows the lives of some members of the London guild of shoemakers. It shows their day-to-day existence being affected by the intimate details of their marital status, pay, and working conditions, as much as by larger events such as the wars being waged by the king in France. Dekker's shoemakers are both marginal to the forces of history and central to the interest of the play. Moreover, their interest lies in their status as a group as much as in their separate individualities. The balance of forces is the opposite of that in *Les Huissiers:* here it is the interweaving of the stories of the shoemakers that takes dramatic precedence over the doings of the nobles—and the duke's son, to enter the game, has to transform himself into a shoemaker too.

In the event the play was produced not by Vilar but by Georges Wilson, in circumstances not conducive to its success. Vilar failed to understand the innovative quality of Vinaver's adaptation; he was preoccupied by the political uncertainties of the time and felt that a national theater such as the T.N.P. had a duty to reaffirm its faith in democracy by making unambiguous statements (in the next two seasons he went on to produce Sophocles' *Antigone,* Aristophanes' *Peace,* Brecht's *Arturo Ui,* and Calderón's *The Mayor of Zalamea*). Vinaver's *La Fête du cordonnier* did not fit into this perspective, so Vilar lost interest in the project and asked his assistant, Georges Wilson, to take his place as director. Wilson was unhappy with this arrangement, and so both he and Vinaver suggested that Planchon should be invited to come and do the production as guest director. Vilar wouldn't hear of it, but by this stage it was too late to cancel the performances, because the T.N.P. subscription system led to the season's program being fixed a long time in advance. Unwill-

ingly, Wilson agreed to go ahead but turned the play into a sort of carnavalesque recreation of *Merrie England,* quite missing the evocation of
everyday working lives, which is the strength of Vinaver's text. The result
was a performance of hollow bombast, and it was a flop with the public.

Sensing that the production of *La Fête du cordonnier* was likely to
be a disaster, Vinaver wrote lengthy notes for the production team and
published an article on the play to coincide with its opening. In these
writings (reprinted in *Ecrits sur le théâtre*) we can see him using the
experience of work on Dekker's text to clarify his own vision of the
theater and to arrive at an accurate definition of its originality. He explains
that Dekker's portrayal of working life in Elizabethan London fails to fit
the heroic style of historical drama familiar to the members of the TNP
company who had performed *Richard II:* "One has to admit that at no
point does the play open out onto a broad demonstration of human passions or ideas that change the world. Each successive situation is relatively
ordinary; none has that exceptional character designed to provoke in an
audience the thrill of tragic emotion or liberating laughter" (*Ecrits sur le
théâtre,* 176).[1] He concludes that the play fails to fit the traditional criteria
of the dramatic and so ends his article by posing a question: "Is there
another approach possible for considering works of theater? . . . An approach through which notions of action, dramatic situation, psychological
character study, and dramatic dialogue would lose their traditional meanings or would have to be totally revised?" (177).[2] If the answer to this
question is yes, he argues, then *La Fête du cordonnier* may contribute to
the demolition of received ideas and to the renewal of the function of
theater. This rather large claim was made in the heat of the disappointment
at seeing his work on Dekker's text betrayed by a willfully uncompre-
hending director, and it seems unlikely that the play, however sympathetically directed, would have been able to achieve such a revolution. In
Vinaver's own work, however, we can see just such a radical experimentation with the forms and functions of theater in our society.

By 1959, when Vinaver made a second attempt to capture the political reality of contemporary France in *Iphigénie Hôtel,* he adopted
Dekker's method of decentering the action and took care not to place
major political events at the center of the plot. As he had done with *Les
Coréens,* he chose to situate the action away from French soil—in a tourist
hotel at Mycenae in Greece. The play takes place on three successive
days: 26, 27, and 28 May 1958. These were the dying days of the Fourth

Republic, when the commanders of the French army in Algeria were about to stage a military putsch, only forestalled by parliament accepting de Gaulle's "offer of himself" and voting him full emergency powers. The news of these events filters through to the Iphigenia Hotel in confused and fragmentary form but does not fundamentally affect the action of the play. This concerns the interlocking strands of the lives of hotel staff and clients, each following his or her trajectory and each more or less influenced by the others. The dramatis personae of the original version contained twenty-one characters: ten members of the staff and eleven visitors. In the final version this number has been reduced to seventeen: ten staff and seven visitors.

In the hotel the former owner, a Greek, is dying. The hotel has been bought by a multinational group, whose representative is away. In his absence Alain, the first valet, maneuvers himself into a position of authority. At the same time Alain is engaged in an attempt to woo Pierrette, one of the chambermaids. Pierrette meanwhile engages in a complicated flirtation with Jacques, the young boot boy, who is so overcome when she drops him for Alain that he absconds, leaving a note to say that he has gone to join the paratroopers. Laure, the other chambermaid, struggles to maintain a sisterly relationship with Pierrette, but, as Pierrette becomes closer to Alain, so she grows more distant from Laure, who is left with nothing but her long-standing relationship with Patrocle, the despised Greek muleteer, who continues to hang about the hotel as he did when it was still in Greek hands. Rather as in Chekhov's plays, the development of the action presents a shifting pattern of status games in which now one character now another achieves a position of ascendancy, only to find that an unexpected alliance between two or three different characters reduces his or her advantage to nothing. The guests, too, relate to one another, or fail to, in a constantly shifting pattern of power play. Although the events in France, as well as the story of the house of Atreus, are constantly present in the background, what happens in the hotel never becomes an allegory or symbol for those things. It retains its own specific reality running parallel to those larger events, making it possible to achieve effects of ironic juxtaposition.

It is impossible to give a satisfactory résumé of the play, since the action is not single but plural: the events of the three days would be recounted differently by each of the characters, and each version would be as valid as the next. The excitement of the play lies in the variety of the action taking place on stage. Each character is both instantly recognizable in his or her own particularity and yet at the same time constantly changing in relation to the other characters and to the situation. There are no moments of choral speaking as such, but the dialogue owes much to the method developed in the group scenes with the soldiers in *Les Coréens* or the ushers in *Les Huissiers*. The published text carries an epigraph by Georges Braque:

> Some people say: "What does your picture show?... What?... There's an apple, of course, there's ... I don't know. ... Ah! a plate beside. ..." These people completely fail to see that what is BETWEEN the apple and the plate can be painted too. And, indeed, it seems to me to be just as difficult to paint the in-between as the things themselves. This "in-between" seems to me as important as what they call the "object." It is precisely the relationship between these objects and that of the objects to the "in-between" which constitutes the subject. (*Théâtre I*, 277)[3]

The action of *Iphigénie Hôtel* takes place entirely in the "in-between" spaces of the different actions or stories evoked—both the developments in the arena of international politics and those that are part of the domestic political struggle taking place in the hotel.

Iphigénie Hôtel was published by *Théâtre Populaire* in its first and longest version. A shorter version for the stage was published by Gallimard in 1963. This was prepared for Jean Tasso, a young director who had intended to produce the play but had to abandon it for lack of funds. Several other projects for productions of this play came to nothing. Finally, it was Antoine Vitez who staged the premiere at the Centre Georges Pompidou in 1977. Together he and Vinaver constructed a new stage version, which is the one published in the collected *Théâtre I*. Vitez's production had a considerable success with critics and public alike. It was set on a traverse stage with two enormous doors at either extremity. The various locations in the hotel were suggested with extreme economy, and spaces overlapped or were even superimposed. The production moved with speed and fluidity and was mostly successful in retaining the multidimensional quality of the text. The sense of events conducted in private, behind closed doors, was damaged by the traverse staging, but there was some compensation in the intimacy of contact achieved between actors and audience.

Themes, Situations, Characters

Although the 1950s was a period of formal experiment in Vinaver's work, the most striking quality of his writing from the very beginning is its thematic richness. A great variety of thematic material is packed into these deceptively banal situations and characters: war and peace, work and play, past and present, power, ambition and impotence, love and betrayal—in fact, all of the major themes of the Western dramatic tradition. Unlike so many of his contemporaries, Vinaver did not become locked into a narrow world of obsession or absurdity. Since he was not seeking to create a reality remarkable for its weird or exceptional quality, the whole range of ordinary experience was available to him. The spectator or reader is plunged into this ordinary experience and finds, with the thrill of discovery, themes gradually taking shape.

Because these themes emerge indirectly out of apparently uninteresting situations, the richness of the thematic material takes the spectator/reader by surprise. Herein lies Vinaver's chief originality: his plays are never *about* war or peace or power. They must start, he insists, from what is most banal and everyday—i.e., that which cannot be separated off with a grandiloquent label. The major themes emerge out of the structuring of this material. Because of this, the characteristic mode of action in Vinaver's plays is reactive. His characters seldom take initiatives but are obliged all the time to improvise, to respond to the pressures put on them (pressures that, as often as not, they fail to understand). Vinaver's themes tend to appear in pairs, allowing for an oscillating movement of action and reaction. The theme of war and peace provides a good example. In *Les Coréens* the subject of how the Korean War started or of why it is being fought is hardly mentioned. This is not because the question seemed unimportant to French people at the time: it was hotly debated in papers and political journals; Sartre, for example, published a long diatribe in *Les Temps Modernes*. Rather, it is because the play aims to show how different people in different situations may react differently to the wartime experience.

Among the French soldiers two different reactions are juxtaposed. The first is that of the group that remains together, whose principal attitude is one of self-preservation (though they also exhibit, at times, a broader awareness of the place they occupy). The second is that of Belair, who discovers an enemy quite different from the propaganda image haunting his companions, who succeeds in making human contact, and who, at the end of the play, decides to remain in the Korean village. Several different attitudes emerge among the Korean villagers: concern for survival is a strong element; so too is resentment of the invader, which, in Kim's case, leads him to join the northern army; in some characters there is a determination to achieve peace and reconciliation; others (represented by Ir Won) just want to escape. This complex thematic material relating to notions of hostility or friendship is entirely dramatized through the relationships between the characters. It is never presented by means of a person with a fixed, stable character such as could be summed up in the one word *noble* or *cowardly*. There is, for example, no one character who embodies hostility or aggression. In this way the relation of men and women to their community and to one another becomes a theme in its own right.

Barthes commented that the characters of *Les Coréens* were not "rôles" that could be categorized in individual or political or historical terms: "they are placed deliberately outside the bounds of positivity or negativity: they *are,* in a way that forestalls any recourse to adjectives" (*Théâtre I,* 39).[4] A comparison with structural linguistics suggests itself: just as individual morphemes have no inherent meaning in the Saussurian system but acquire meaning, instead, through a process of differentiation, so the characters of *Les Coréens* take shape only through interplay with one another, in the infinitely complex, never-ending process of agreement and disagreement, assimilation and differentiation. The nature of interpersonal relations thus emerges as a theme. *Les Coréens* proposes a view of the world in which character cannot be separated from relationship because the former emerges only in and through the process that constitutes the latter.

This explains why one of the most frequent recurring themes in Vinaver's theater is that of adherence to, or exclusion from, a group. Both French soldiers and Korean villagers discuss what it is that links them to, or separates them from, their respective groupings. In some cases the answer can be established quite simply. Mio-Wan, for example, is in no doubt that he and the other villagers have a duty to feed "their" army. Almost everyone agrees with this, except for Ir-Won, who, because of this fundamental difference of opinion, quite literally separates himself from the other members of his community. By a supreme irony it is he who will be captured by the French and taken back to their headquarters in the guise of a northern soldier. In other cases the matter is not so simply settled. When Lhomme and Lhorizon have decided to take the dead Koreans' clothes in order to move through the bush in disguise, they find it necessary to discuss their former occupations in French civilian life so as to overcome their sense of betraying their group identity.

All of Vinaver's early plays are structured on a double opposition: there is opposition between two differently constituted groups, and there is opposition between those who are part of the group and those who are not. The latter may be excluded willingly or unwillingly; occasionally, someone will move from one group to another, a difficult transition successfully accomplished by only one character: Belair in *Les Coréens*. In this play the scenes between the small group of French soldiers cut off in the Korean bush have all the veracity and tension that we have since come to recognize from films depicting Americans caught in hostile Vietnamese territory. There is no point of contact whatever between their concerns, interests, and needs and those of the Korean villagers wondering how to rebuild their bombed homes. The two groups are separated by less than a mile of ground, but they might as well be on two different continents. Belair's detachment from the group is provoked by the death of a wounded American soldier. There are two phases to the detachment. The first is the negative phase: in the brief conversation he has with the American before his death Belair becomes aware of the enormous distance separating them, although they are "on the same side." The second phase is the positive one, when Wen-Ta, a Korean child, appears, and Belair realizes that he is able to communicate with her, that they share the same concerns. The group's tendency to self-perpetuation is strong and is constantly reinforced by the evocation of a threatening external force. But once separated from the group the individual becomes more open to influence from the outside.

The contrast between soldiers and villagers in *Les Coréens* relies on an opposition between different attitudes toward the value of a human life: the author's sympathy for the villagers is evident, perhaps at times too evident. It emerges in the contrast between the treatment meted out to aliens by the villagers on the one hand and the soldiers on the other. The soldiers capture a young Korean whom they suspect of planting mines; they treat him with indifference or contempt, and, when they have to move on, they shoot him. The villagers, on the other hand, accept Belair (albeit after some hesitation), see his needs as a human being, and make attempts to meet them. But these elements of value judgment do not prevent Vinaver from depicting with great complexity and in compelling detail the different social processes that go to make for the cohesion of a group of villagers or a group of soldiers. The play of opposition and contrasts encourages us not to judge and to criticize (as Brechtian drama does) but to suspend judgment and to understand.

In the other early plays the groups are less clearly opposed, and the emphasis lies more on the relationship between groups and individuals. In *Les Huissiers,* for example, the group of ushers remains homogenous throughout; it is not really opposed to the group of politicians. The action of the play lies in the constantly shifting pattern of inclusion and exclusion among the politicians. The one moment of sharp dramatic conflict in the play occurs in the interview between Paidoux and Mme Aiguedon. She retains a singleness and purity of purpose that has long since deserted the politicians. The result is that they no longer speak the same language: Mme Aiguedon, by rejecting their mentality, excludes herself from their group and, therefore, from achieving what she wants but also shows them up for what they are. In *La Fête du cordonnier* we see this opposition reversed and played out in a comic key: Lacy, the young aristocrat, dresses up as a shoemaker in order to further his amorous intrigue with the Lord Mayor's daughter. Despite his evident inauthenticity, he manages to get himself accepted by the company of honest-minded shoemakers, whereupon some of their authenticity rubs off on him: his amorous pursuit is changed from an aristocrat's whim into a true love, consecrated at the end of the play by marriage.

It is in *Iphigénie Hôtel* that the theme of group identity is explored with the greatest complexity, since Alain's campaign to assume power depends a great deal on his ability to handle group dynamics (as well as the administration of the hotel). In the seventh scene, strongly reminiscent of the scenes set in the servants' quarters in Renoir's *La Règle du jeu,* we see Alain carefully playing off one member of the staff against another, mixing dominating and conciliatory behavior in such a way as to assure his mastery of the group. Patrocle, the only Greek among them, is used particularly ruthlessly to emphasize that continued membership of the group will only be permitted on condition of obedience to him, Alain. Through his treatment of the theme of group identity Vinaver generates a great deal of suspense in performance. The audience becomes drawn into the game and shares the uncertainties of the different characters as they struggle for inclusion or escape. This emotional participation by the audience is not, however, the hypnotic identification condemned by Brecht: Vinaver's spectator acquires a lucid understanding of the social mechanisms at work and is never allowed to remain for long with a single viewpoint—the constant alternation of scenes sees to that.

In *Iphigénie Hôtel*, for example, the scenes follow a regular pattern of alternation between the staff quarters and the hotel's public rooms, occupied by the clients. The scenes with the clients introduce concerns of such a distant nature (the archaeology of Mycenae, the events of 13 May in France, etc.) that the intrigues "below stairs" are thrown into comic relief. At the same time casual relationships are formed and broken off between the clients, in contrast to which the struggle for power among the staff stands out in all its seriousness. This is because the author has woven into his story of life below stairs the themes of power and ambition resonant with historical precedents (Agamemnon) and contemporary politics (de Gaulle). The play was written immediately after de Gaulle's spectacular return to power, when there was still a great uncertainty about whether he was simply playing power games or whether he was genuinely able to control the political forces in such a way as to reunite the country. The same ambiguity characterizes the depiction of Alain. At first he seems to be going through the motions without being capable of exercizing real authority. But by the end of the play he is beginning to grow into his new post, and this is connected with his success in persuading Pierrette to marry him. In this way the theme of love is tied in with the theme of ambition.

A similar relation between the themes of love and ambition can be seen in *Les Huissiers*, where Paidoux's success in rehabilitating himself with the party that has rejected him is due, in part, to Mme Tigon, his secretary and mistress. Where the linked treatment of these two themes was partly derisory in *Iphigénie Hôtel*, in *Les Huissiers* it is wholly so. The play evokes the slow disintegration of the bravery and passion of the Resistance years in the aimless decade that followed. Paidoux has a glorious past, but his former faith and energy have disappeared to the point where he is merely going through the motions of holding onto power. When the play opens he appears to be losing his grip; by the end he has regained it.

Seeking for a way to bring out the unreal nature of the arguments apparently separating the politicians of the Fourth Republic, Vinaver decided to adopt what he called a neutral structure: that of *Oedipus at Colonus*. Thus, the exiled Oedipus becomes Paidoux, and the faithful Antigone Mme Tigon. Vinaver hoped that the antics of the politicians would emerge in a suitably ridiculous light since their essential emptiness would contrast with the plenitude of Sophocles' tragedy. But he was caught in a trap, for no structure is neutral. The structure of *Oedipus at Colonus* was conceived to express the transformation that may occur when a man who has passed through great suffering and caused terrible disasters acquires, at the end of his life, a numinous quality to which people are attracted and which they seek to appropriate for themselves. It is not a structure that is able to sustain the opposite trajectory: that of a man who has lost such power and has become simply a "fixer."

This in turn throws an interesting light on Vinaver's method of character construction. The first four plays all have large casts and distribute the lines fairly evenly among the different characters. This means that there can be relatively little character study of the kind represented, for example, by Gide's Oedipus or by Sartre's Kean. Vinaver's dramatis personae have been called "figures" rather than "personages," profiles rather than characters. This is perhaps an unjust judgment on the playwright's ability to create instantly recognizable people, having the stamp of characters we have all known. It is, however, true to say that all Vinaver's individuals are defined in relation to other individuals or to groups. The system of oppositions analyzed above is what generates the audience's sense of recognizing a given personality, whose language, habits of thought, or action take on their particular profile in contrast to many others, some quite similar, others very different. This is why the most successful plays are those with the maximum interplay of different characters, such as *Iphigénie Hôtel.* In *Les Huissiers* the ushers, though very successful as a group, are entirely separate from the group of politicians and secretaries, whereas the latter are indistinguishable to the point of being almost interchangeable. Apart from the brief challenge by Mme Aiguedon there is no room for the interplay of differentiation that makes up the richness of character and language in Vinaver's other plays.

Commitment and *L'Objecteur*

In France in the 1950s the question of the political responsibility of the writer was very high on the agenda. At the beginning of the decade Sartre and Camus had conducted an extended public argument about how far literature could or should become committed. It was the period of the last of France's colonial wars and of the *Manifesto of the 121,* signed by a group of writers and intellectuals in protest against French policy in Algeria. It was also the period in which the French theater "discovered" Brecht and the possibility of a theater that was both politically committed and artistically complex. In such an atmosphere it was natural for any new writer to be scrutinized closely for traces of political commitment, and the scrutiny applied to Vinaver was especially close in view of his choice of subject matter. Camus had already commented on Vinaver's unusual position in relation to the problems of the writer's commitment (see page 9). His suggestion was that Vinaver exhibited a kind of commitment that could not be categorized according to the then accepted criteria. In very different terms Roland Barthes expressed a similar thought in his review of *Les Coréens* (then entitled *Aujourd'hui*) for the weekly *France-Observateur*. Discussing the nature of Belair's progress in the course of the play, he considered that:

> In fact, we witness neither a choice nor a conversion nor an act of desertion but, rather, a gradual act of consent as the soldier acquiesces in the Korean reality that he discovers. . . . What this lost soldier says yes to is not a new "order," not an ideology, not a cause, it is a shared bowl of rice. . . . So is *Aujourd'hui* a political play? No, if by political is meant speeches, professions of faith, doctrine. . . . Vinaver's characters never talk politics. Yes, absolutely yes, if politics consists in rediscovering real relationships between human beings stripped of all psychological "embellishments." . . . Is this realist theater? No, but it is objective theater, as far removed from Zhdanovian preachifying as it is from bourgeois psychologizing; and this view of the real is something new, I believe, in our French theater. (Cited in Ubersfeld, *Vinaver dramaturge*, 15)[5]

The quality in Vinaver's work admired by both Camus and Barthes is something that they find hard to describe but could be loosely summed up as a "commitment to the real." It consistently and carefully avoids all the established political clichés in an attempt to reach at what lies behind political doctrines of all schools: the attempt to define how human beings should relate to one another in social groupings. Camus's own attempt to reach such a "view of the real" started with the negative analysis of the individual's sense of alienation, in *L'Etranger,* before moving on to the more positive affirmation of human solidarity to be found in *La Peste.* In Vinaver's case a similar progression can be observed between his novel *L'Objecteur* and his first play. Both works contain a character who is alienated by the existing systems of social organization and who seek, in Barthes's words, "to rediscover the real relationships between human beings." The first, Bême, ends in self-destruction; the second, Belair, ends in self-affirmation.

The term *objecteur* was carefully chosen by Vinaver as the title of his novel. It suggests a conscientious objector (the French term is *objecteur de conscience*), but, by only including half of the phrase, he leaves a certain ambiguity, lending the term a more general applicability. Bême, like Belair, is someone whose action will be described by the French army as desertion. But, strictly speaking, he is neither a deserter nor a conscientious objector, since his behavior follows no predetermined plan. He is a young man called up on National Service who, one day on the parade ground, makes an act of passive resistance. He sits on the ground and takes no notice of further orders. The key to understanding Bême as *objecteur* lies in his similarity to Meursault, Camus's *étranger*. Like Meursault, Bême possesses a heightened sense of the value of commonplace or everyday events. He responds in a direct way to the physical demands of the moment, unmediated by thoughts of career or the subsequent consequences of his actions. Like Meursault's, Bême's resistance to the established order of things has both its negative and its positive poles. On the negative side it is instinctive and, therefore, potentially destructive. On the positive side it stems from a deeply felt response to lived experience and the sincere attempt to be true to that experience.

In one passage of *L'Objecteur* Vinaver directly addresses the problem of commitment in literature and links it to this need to be true to lived experience. This comes in a discussion between Lecorre, a history teacher, and Barboux, a philosopher. The philosopher claims that, if commitment means anything, it is the necessary consequence of knowledge and is, for that reason, unavoidable. He alludes to the debate on literature and commitment, insisting that it is all a gigantic joke: "One cannot help being committed the moment one knows something. Conversely, any commitment which is not based on knowledge is like a magic spell and harmful to the organism" (*L'Objecteur*, 69).[6] The context of this discussion is the suggestion that commitment must necessarily be part of a dynamic relationship between the individual and his or her situation and will therefore depend on the individual's knowledge and understanding of that situation. The situation may be one in which it is possible to intervene effectively, but it may be one in which only a "negative commitment" is possible—in other words, in which the only honest stance available is that of *l'objecteur*.

L'objecteur thus shares with Camus's Meursault a keen eye for the hypocrisies of day-to-day behavior and an attempt to live without the familiar life props that preserve the comfortable sense that our lives have structure and meaning. He places the highest value on immediate, physical sensation and tries to be true to this. In *L'Objecteur* the history teacher remembers that Bême, when he was a schoolboy, had an unusual approach to the study of history: profound indifference to the "great events" (battles, invasions, etc.) but a passionate interest in the details of everyday life at different periods. When Belair, in *Les Coréens,* finds himself cut off from his company and from the battle to separate the North and South Korean armies, he enters a world of which, as yet, he knows nothing and so can only trust his immediate experience. He finds that his familiar preconceptions fall away and that he begins to understand his situation quite differently because he is freed from the categories normally imposed on his life. Instead of fighting, regrouping, following the normal imperatives of army discipline, he sits still, looks around, learns from the situation, construes it differently from the way he has previously been taught to.

In his note on Vinaver's attitude toward commitment Camus had understood that, although Vinaver's approach to literature was the opposite of the cold war militancy advocated by Sartre, this did not mean that he denied the necessity for a close relationship between the fictional world of literature and the real world of everyday experience. Quite the reverse: Vinaver wished to recreate in his work something of the complexity of the real world. It was his success in achieving this that Barthes responded to and struggled so hard to analyze: "The originality of the work is, paradoxically, to be situated, as it were, in pre-ideological territory, without this ever becoming an irresponsible solution. . . . A new kind of accommodation with reality is being proposed," one that escapes the Manichaeism of much French literature of the period, "as if there were no other aesthetic solution to human ills apart from Order or Protest" (*Théâtre I,* 37–38).[7] Vinaver's ability to stake out this "pre-ideological territory" in his early plays shows him still, to some extent, marked by the mental structures of Camus's existentialism. But in the figure of *l'objecteur,* especially in the form of Belair, he defines an original stance: passive resistance to received hierarchies and an openness to reality that will be the basis of all his subsequent work. It is a view of reality that he was to define, many years later, when talking of Erdman: "A view that is passive, not committed, receptive, combining clemency and irony, tenderness and bite" (32).[8]

NOTES

1. Force est de constater qu'aucun moment de la pièce ne débouche sur la manifestation large des passions humaines, ou des idées qui transforment le monde. Chacune des situations qui se succèdent est relativement quelconque; aucune n'a ce caractère à la fois exceptionnel et exemplaire qui provoque chez le spectateur la vibration génératrice de l'émotion tragique ou du rire libérateur.

2. Existe-t-il une optique différente, à partir de laquelle une pièce de théâtre puisse être considérée? . . . Une optique à l'intérieur de laquelle les notions d'action, de situation dramatique, de psychologie des personnages et de langage théâtral n'auraient aucun sens ou demanderaient à être entièrement révisées?

3. Il y a des gens qui disent: "Que représente votre tableau? . . . Quoi? . . . Il y a une pomme, c'est entendu, il y a . . . Je ne sais pas . . . Ah! une assiette; à côté. . . ." Ces gens-là ont l'air d'ignorer totalement que ce qui est ENTRE la pomme et l'assiette se peint aussi. Et, ma foi, il me paraît tout aussi difficile de peindre l'entre-deux que les choses. Cet "entre-deux" me paraît un élément aussi capital que ce qu'ils appellent "l'objet." C'est justement le rapport de ces objets entre eux et de l'objet avec "l'entre-deux" qui constitue le sujet.

4. Ils sont délibérément au-delà ou en deçà de la positivité et de la négativité: ils *sont,* coupant ainsi tout recours à l'adjectif.

5. En fait, nous n'assistons ni à un choix, ni à une conversion, ni à une désertion, mais plutôt à un assentiment progressif: le soldat acquiesce au monde coréen qu'il découvre. . . . Ce à quoi le soldat perdu dit oui, ce n'est pas à un "ordre" nouveau, à une idéologie, à une cause, c'est à la soupe commune (le riz: c'est très important.) . . . Est-ce qu'*Aujourd'hui* est une pièce politique? Non, si la politique, c'est le discours, la profession de foi, la thèse. . . : les personnages de Vinaver ne parlent jamais sur la politique. Oui, pleinement oui, si la politique consiste à retrouver les rapports réels des hommes débarrassés de toute "décoration" psychologique. . . . Est-ce un théâtre réaliste? Non, mais c'est un théâtre objectif, aussi éloigné en cela du préchi-précha jdanovien que du psychologisme bourgeois; et cette vue du réel est quelque chose de nouveau, je crois dans notre théâtre français.

6. Gigantesque rigolade! Nécessairement on s'engage à partir du moment où l'on connaît. Inversement tout engagement qui n'est pas basé sur une prise de connaissance est un acte magique, néfaste à l'organisme.

7. La nouveauté de l'oeuvre, c'est, paradoxalement, de se situer dans un certain *en-deçà* des concepts idéologiques, sans pourtant jamais faire de cette restriction une irresponsabilité. . . . C'est un nouveau type d'accommodement au réel qui est proposé. Comme s'il n'y avait d'autre issue esthétique aux malheurs humains que l'Ordre ou la Protestation.

8. Un regard passif, non engagé, disponible, où se combinent clémence et ironie, tendresse et morsure. (The word *disponible* was used by Gide to convey openness to whatever opportunities life puts in one's way.)

Chapter 3

Overboard

For most of the 1960s Vinaver appeared to have abandoned play writing. His work at Gillette took up more of his time; he was traveling around Europe from one posting to another. Nevertheless, it was in the middle of this period that he wrote one of his longest and most important articles on the theater. The article, published in *Théâtre Populaire,* was an analysis of Planchon's production of *Troilus and Cressida,* ranging widely across the triple themes of contemporary theater production, Shakespearean theater, and ancient Greek mythology. Through these reflections we can see Vinaver clarifying the problems that were to confront him when he once again began to write for the theater.

Planchon's production of *Troilus and Cressida* had met with considerable hostility from the critics; Vinaver's first concern was to establish why. Having attended the production on two separate nights, he concluded that the explanation lay in the originality of Planchon's approach to Shakespeare. The production was different from anything he had done before and different from the way in which the French were used to seeing Shakespeare performed. On his first visit Vinaver wrote that he too had been confused and had experienced a reflex of boredom. He argued that boredom is not necessarily caused by the artistic inadequacy of the performance; it may also be a natural defense aroused in the spectator unable to achieve any purchase on something totally new to him. On his second visit, possessing a basic familiarity with the play and the production, he was able to appreciate it in quite a different way. Having identified the broad thrust of play and production, he was able to enter into a relationship with it, to follow with agreement or disagreement, to experience the action as a succession of "crossroads of possibilities," each giving rise to expectation, hope, or fear.

The play had confused him because, though taking the most traditional themes and situation (love and war at Troy), it treats them in a completely unexpected manner. Planchon's production had added to this confusion by using language and movement that were abrupt, modern, the opposite of the lyrical or the heroic mode that audiences had come to associate with Shakespeare from Jean Vilar's productions. But on his second visit Vinaver began to see in the play "an exceptional freedom," and his account could also be read as a summary of his own ambitions as a writer: "Its development seems almost improvised, displaying a sovereign indifference for the expected links in the action. . . . There is not a single moment when what happens is what had to happen. Each instant is absolute. The constant contradictions and breaks in the meaning are reinforced by constant discrepancies of tone" (*Ecrits sur le théâtre,* 96).[1] This was particularly striking since Shakespeare was using the best known of all mythical material, the Trojan wars. Vinaver expresses his admiration for Shakespeare's ability to dispense with all the idealistic treatment of this subject matter—i.e., the glorifications of love and war—and to achieve instead what he calls "cette absolue plénitude de l'instant présent" (this fullness of the present moment). He goes on to identify very clearly the quality of the play that had made Planchon want to produce it. At this time Planchon was emerging from his Brechtian phase and searching for a form of theater equally powerful in its depiction of social process but less dependent on didactic story. He had begun to write his own plays in which, like Brecht, he modeled his work on that of the Elizabethans. *Troilus and Cressida,* wrote Vinaver, "opened up a theater freed from the constraints of story line, explosively open to every possibility, rich in limitless resonances, informing contemporary reality without didactic closure" (97).[2] This was to prove an accurate assessment of the direction in which Vinaver's own dramaturgical experiments would develop.

Vinaver suggested a term to designate the dramatic method Planchon was reaching for: "a rigorously descriptive theater" *(un théâtre rigoureusement descriptif),* but one whose function is not so much to illustrate as to *reveal:* "As an instrument of investigation, it has the power to bring us face to face with the unexpected aspects of ourselves" (*Ecrits sur le théâtre,* 102).[3] This, he argued, was what Shakespeare had achieved in *Troilus and Cressida* because of the particular use he made of his mythical material. He saw a close parallel with the way the Athenian dramatists of the fifth century b.c. had used the same material: to question and to test accepted truths by presenting the familiar myths quite *differ-*

ently—if necessary, presenting them in almost unrecognizable form in order to challenge the received ideas of the audience. So he concluded that, as in musical composition, successful dramatic writing depends on both repetition and variation. The play must *repeat* material already known to the audience so as to permit its members some purchase on it, but then it must *vary* that material so as to confront them with the unexpected and thus to achieve the effect of revelation. Vinaver distinguished this from Brechtian theater, whose purpose was to serve a unified ideological explanation of the world, but insisted that this did not imply an apolitical stance: simply because a play refused to present its material judgmentally did not mean that it could have no political force. On the contrary, a careful description of the warp and weft of history was the first condition for political action with any real purchase on today's world. This line of argument brought him back to considerations of form: "As soon as it is no longer a question of convincing, but of describing, formal problems reassert themselves. For the content of the description cannot be separated from the manner in which the description is set out. The distinction between form and content disappears" (107).[4]

Par-dessus bord marked the coming to fruition in Vinaver's own practice as a playwright of what he had called "a rigorously descriptive theater." As we have seen, this term designated a theater not illustrating a key philosophy or seeking to persuade us of a particular interpretation of the world but a theater giving consistency to the world through the interplay of different interpretations. This notion of descriptive theater implies its own peculiar problems of structure, which can be expressed as follows: If Vinaver, as author, selects and arranges the material, then is it not, inevitably, patterned and shaped by his own philosophy? In *Iphigénie Hôtel* he had solved this problem by borrowing his structure and much of his material from another source. With *Par-dessus bord* this solution was excluded. His motive for undertaking the play was to find a way of bringing together his two separate selves: Michel Grinberg the business executive and Michel Vinaver the writer. He therefore adopted the characteristically Modernist device of incorporating his own uncertainties and divisions into the work: he included a character whose position reproduced his own—that is to say, he is both an executive with the firm and a writer. As the play unfolds, this character develops a meditation on the problems confronting him as he tries to write a play about the firm. He uses the form, unusual in Vinaver's theater, of direct address to the audience, whose members soon come to realize that the play he is discussing is the same one that they are watching. By this device the very process of dramatic creation, especially the near impossibility of staging satisfactorily the complexities of a large commercial enterprise, become a significant element of the play, at the structural as well as the thematic level. The audience is invited to join the playwright in a meditation on the central question of how we may best make images or tell stories or recreate the world so as to understand and act upon it.

The interventions of the author figure, named Passemar, are treated in a manner reminiscent of Aristophanes: what he discusses is serious enough, but he himself is a buffoon, and his comments are always interrupted by others pushing him aside. They challenge him on his own ground, however, since they are themselves concerned with similar preoccupations about the problem of how to represent the world. They include a group of dancers choreographing a performance that is to be based on Norse myths; Alex, a jazz player, whose music becomes an integral part of several scenes; and the company boss, who is also an amateur painter. As well as showing these practitioners at work, the play contains a running meditation on the nature and function of group encounters, parties, happenings of all kinds ("happenings" were much in vogue at the time).

As with the theme of artistic process, so with all the other themes of the play, the structural principle employed by Vinaver is to bring together as many different approaches as possible in such a way as to allow for the maximum richness of texture and resonance to derive from their interweaving. This would be an extremely haphazard program if it had no anchorage in a defined situation, hence the importance of the commercial enterprise within whose organization every separate episode or character is linked to every other. The choice of *which* company was crucial: it had to have real significance within the French economy while at the same time offering theatrically exciting possibilities. Vinaver decided on a toilet paper manufacturer with the respectable name of Ravoire & Dehaze. This company became the nexus of the dramatic action. Charles Joris, in a program note for his production, wrote that "the hero is the company of Ravoire & Dehaze, or a character one could name 'Radé.' The various characters of the play—about fifty in all—are simply living functions within the great body of Radé" ("Une Comédie des pouvoirs," 14). The success of Vinaver's interweaving process is partly due to the constant switching from the level of macrocosm, the large institutional body of Radé (will it survive? in what form? how can its existence be defined, influenced, related to?), to the level of microcosm, the separate individual existences that go to make up Radé. In the constant come and go between these two levels he developed an extended commentary on how far the individuals depend on Radé and how far it depends on them. Between these two there is a constant tension embodied most acutely in the character of Passemar, both an executive in the firm and the author of the play we are watching. Through this character Vinaver expresses his pain at having to bring together the private world of creative writing and the public world of commercial enterprise but also the liberation that this ultimately brings him.

At the macrocosmic level, that of the commercial enterprise, a strong story line develops in the epic mode. It follows the fortunes of this old-fashioned French family firm as it begins to feel the cold wind of competition from the United States. Each of the play's six "movements" shows the firm at a different phase in its development. The first movement presents the state of the market at the outset, as the American "softies" make their first challenge. In the second movement Ravoire & Dehaze decide to counter with an improved hard paper in a *bleu-blanc-rouge* wrapper, but the French do not respond to this call to patriotism, continuing to buy the new American product. The head of the Dehaze family, who is also the firm's managing director, collapses with a heart attack. In the third movement the firm's sales have dropped drastically; a large bank loan has to be negotiated, and this opens the way to a fight for the succession between the two half-brothers Olivier and Benoit. The fourth movement shows Benoit, the illegitimate brother, triumphantly introducing American consultants and imposing new psychoanalytic methods in their approach to advertising and sales strategies. In the fifth movement this tactic has paid off, and the firm's own new brand of soft paper has captured a major share of the market, but in the sixth and final movement the American challenger abandons the fight, deciding instead to buy up Ravoire & Dehaze as a profitable subsidiary.

At the microcosmic level (i.e., within each of these movements, or miniplays) the audience's interest is engaged by a variety of interwoven personal dramas. There is, for example, the drama of Margerie, the American wife of the old boss's illegitimate son Benoit; she loses interest in her husband as she sees him changing from a carefree young man into the new boss. Instead, she seduces his legitimate brother Olivier, who is too gentlemanly to prevent control of the firm slipping from his grasp. Or again there is the drama of Lubin, one of the sales staff (who loses his job in the course of the shake-up) and of his daughter Geneviève, who is determined to marry Alex the jazzman and who succeeds. Lubin opens the play in dialogue with Mme Lepine, a retailer, on one of his regular visits. In this dialogue Vinaver has captured with deadly accuracy the peculiar relationship that exists between the two parties to a commercial transaction. Part of the dialogue is extremely personal: each party asks after the other's family with real concern; there is room here for genuine exchange of human emotion. But at any moment this is liable to tip over into a different kind of dialogue, one in which each speaker adopts a self-conscious role, clearly recognized by the other, and at this point Lubin's attempt to make a sale becomes a kind of trial of strength, or jousting match.

Within each of the separate movements (at this microcosmic level) Vinaver makes use of suspense and uncertainty about the direction of the market, the fortunes of the company, the choices that have to be faced. The dominant mood at any given moment is confusion and fragmentation; it is only in the course of the long-term development of the play's action (seven hours of playing time uncut) that the firm's trajectory becomes clear. As the drama unfolds, moment by moment, we are interested in the private, individual dramas as much as in the public, corporate story. The originality of Vinaver's method, the particular rhythm that he is fond of alluding to, does not consist merely in presenting two kinds of drama, the private and the public. It lies in the method of interweaving these two things, and this has to be shown by detailed reference to a section of the play. We will choose part of the fourth movement, running in the 1972 L'Arche edition on pages 121–55 (an abbreviated version appears in *Théâtre I*, 443–58).

Analysis: Fourth Movement—Moss and Heather

The section opens with Passemar alone on stage addressing the audience. This speech corresponds to the Aristophanic *parabasis*, in which the chorus would speak on behalf of the playwright. Aristophanes used these passages to comment on his difficulties as an author and to defend himself from accusations. He did not employ the device (in the manner of Brecht) to comment on or correct our understanding of the story. Vinaver's intervention is similar to Aristophanes's, a similarity underlined by the entrance of the dancers who overwhelm his attempt at Apollonian reason with Dionysian action. Passemar's comments are also reminiscent of the authorial intrusions by Gide in *Les Caves du Vatican*—questioning the direction that his play should take, wondering how to integrate the different elements. At the same time there is a ludicrous side to his situation, rather as if he were an old music hall comedian forced off the stage before he can finish his act by lively young dancers; finding they cannot get rid of him, they incorporate him into their routine. As Passemar tries to articulate his embarrassment concerning the scatological elements of his story, the dancers are attempting to rehearse a ballet of the death of Baldr. One of them mimes the casting of the mistletoe spear, and Passemar falls.

This passage superimposes a number of conflicts of different orders. First, there is the fundamental tension experienced in the mind of the author about his role as a writer in the context of the business world: his *personal* reluctance in the face of the subject matter ("Tout ce qui est grossier m'est personnellement pénible" [Anything at all coarse causes me personal discomfort]) is an expression of his fundamental uneasiness at bringing together his two lives—that of the businessman and that of the author. Second, there is a conflict between him and the dancers about which will succeed in capturing the stage space (and the audience's attention). Then there is the conflict of the different stories: Passemar is trying to tell the story of the triumph of American marketing methods; the dancers are trying to tell the story of the death of Baldr and of the struggle between the Ases and the Vanes. In Norse mythology Baldr was the god who was loved by everyone, whose judgments were always good, but whose advice could never be put into practice. His death at the hands of Loki marked the triumph of evil over good; it seemed a total disaster. Yet it was followed by an unexpected reconciliation of the warring parties and a renewal of life and hope. This ancient version of the myth of death and resurrection stands in contrast to the brash story of the American attack on the French market. The two stories are placed in a relationship of maximum tension: they seem to have nothing whatever to do with one another. If any connections are made, they seem quite incongruous: Passemar having to stand in for Baldr, for example. But the tension and incongruity is compensated or counteracted by a unifying movement at the thematic level: the theme of hostility giving way to reconciliation gradually emerges as the shared element.

This scene is followed by a group encounter in which the American marketing consultants seek to expose the natural taboos of the French personnel when it comes to discussing shit. This section runs uninterrupted for eight pages. It is an intensely dramatic scene and functions as a microcosm of the whole play, since it embodies conflict, crisis, and reconciliation at a number of levels. The Americans choose to pitch their first meeting with the executives of Ravoire & Dehaze at the level of an all-out attack. Having been invited in to solve the firm's problems, they are in a position of power, which they use in order to force the French to confront their own embarrassment: they intend to pass like a dose of salts through the corporate body of Radé. They diagnose its problem as a sort of mental and organizational constipation: the executives will have to learn to "let go" psychologically in order to come to terms with the pleasure of "letting go" physically; only then will they be in a position to develop the correct marketing strategy. The scene is hilarious but also very tense: some of the executives are prepared to enter into the consultants' game, while others are upset by their confrontational approach. One (Peyre) puts up a total resistance, finally walking out of the room and slamming the door behind him. But what had been experienced as an aggressive challenge soon shifts into a more conciliatory analysis of individual responses: Peyre is brought back into the room, and a new harmony is achieved. In the course of this scene the audience shares the suspense that is built up, both within the group of executives and within themselves, as fundamental taboos are tested.

The scene also forms a stage in the larger conflict enacted in the play: the struggle for control of the French toilet paper market. All the conflicting elements are resolved in an ironic perspective as everyone agrees on the primordial importance of marketing. The anguish aroused by having to confront taboo subjects is soothed by a solemn affirmation culminating in Passemar's "C'est la création" (It's creativity) and Benoit's reply: "C'est la vie" (It's life) (132). The ironic perspective is underlined in the following two pages as Jack Donohue reads his "tables of the law." The effect is somewhat similar to the *maximes du mariage* (maxims of marriage) that are read out in Molière's play *L'Ecole des femmes;* by giving exaggerated importance to the subject under discussion (marketing or marriage), the list of laws ends up by making it seem ridiculous. The comedy here inflates the ironic procedure to the dimensions of Aristophanic farce: Jack Donohue starts from the assertion that "people's needs are limited in number, but, since their desires and fears are limitless, marketing's job is to make them proliferate." This leads him to the conclusion that a marketing man must be everything at once: a lover, a warrior, a creator, a destroyer, etc., and he must be prepared to possess, penetrate, even rape the client (in a metaphorical sense). The absurd disproportion between such terms and the object of the exercise (to increase sales of toilet paper) produces a profoundly comic result.

Immediately following this comes an interview between Passemar and Benoit, the illegitimate son of the former managing director, who has now taken control of the firm. This too is a highly comic scene, relying not on conflict of character but of two different languages. Benoit and Passemar have a discussion on which no personal hostility is manifested, rather the opposite, but in which Benoit's manipulation of the tough marketing jargon learned from the Americans drives Passemar to retrench, falling back into the feudal terminology of the old-fashioned family firm.

Lubin then appears, asking to speak to Cohen, the firm's accountant, and this is followed by a brief dialogue between Margerie and Topfer. Topfer was the antique dealer who supplied the dead Mr. Dehaze with many of the best items in his collection of eighteenth-century snuff boxes. Margerie has come to him because she, too, is interested in these collector's items. Indeed, she is preparing a thesis for her American university on "precious objects in the development of court politics between 1740 and 1769." Topfer shows her a box painted with a licentious picture, which evokes, he says, the Marquis de Sade. This conversation continues for five more pages, intercut with the scene in the Ravoire & Dehaze office where the executives are waiting for Jack Donohue to arrive for a brainstorming session. Themes of possession, of penetration and of anality, hover in the background of both discussions, commenting by association of ideas and ironic juxtaposition on the links between pleasure, possession, and profit. Topfer's encomium on the late Mr. Dehaze's erudition is placed side by side with Peyre's admiring account of Jack Donohue's meteoric career in marketing. The theme of instrumentality of desire is raised by Topfer's evocation of Mme de Pompadour procuring fresh young flesh for Louis XV, while Battestini encourages his colleagues to associate freely around ideas of innocence and pleasure. Margerie is excited by the new snuff box, says she *must* have it.

There follow six pages of hilarious brainstorming, in which 187 different names are suggested for the new brand of toilet paper, ranging from the sublime to the ridiculous. Perhaps it would be more accurate to say that they combine both sublime and ridiculous. "Ecstacy, Apotheosis, Hosannah, Excelsior [*Extase, Apothéose, Hosannah, Excelsior*]" all have connotations with the sublime, but in the context of the dramatic situation appear quintessentially ridiculous. In a different way "Golden Fleece,

My Pleasure, Golden Sands, Virgin Vine, Gentle Breeze [*Toison d'or, Mon Plaisir, Sable d'or, Vigne vierge, Brise légère*] are comic by association. The comedy is further emphasized when we reflect that the whole purpose of the session is supposed to be the search for a name that will function in just the same way—i.e., by association—in persuading shoppers to part with their money. Vinaver's dramaturgical method, too, proceeds by association. The process of inventing the name—Moss and Heather *(Mousse et Bruyère)* is the final choice—is not presented as *essentially* ridiculous. Drawing on the theories of Freud, Reich, and others, it is genuinely revealing about our common mental and imaginative processes. That is what gives it dramatic power and conviction. What is ridiculous is that such a deployment of creative energy should be expended on something so essentially trivial as a sales drive for this product. Added comedy is derived from the *deceptive* element involved, since the advertiser is seeking to touch off the right associations without revealing too much; the dramatist, on the other hand, aims to reveal exactly how such associations function, to lay bare the whole process.

This part of the text is written in a form that suggests choral speaking, the lines not attributed to named speakers. After the 187th suggestion it cuts immediately to a scene between Lubin and Cohen. All the preceding sections had been centered around suppressed desires to do with possessing, penetrating, letting go, etc.; this scene continues the same thematic material in a completely different register. Lubin is worried about losing possession of his daughter. He is especially worried that she has taken up with a Jew. He can think of nothing better than to ask Cohen to find out something about him, since he imagines that "all Jews are more or less in contact with one another." Here again, just as in the scene between Passemar and Benoit, the relations between the two men remain entirely proper: at the level appropriate to a dialogue between two employees. But their language reveals tension and opposition. In Lubin's words we recognize what Sarrazac calls "a linguistic impulse" *(une poussée du langage)* (see page 7), revealing all the underlying assumptions of traditional French anti-Semitism. The scene then cuts back to the post-brainstorming discussion in which Jenny displays a more patronizing, Anglo Saxon type of racism, as she alludes to "those Negro fetishes which I just adore—I have made a really cute collection of them."[5] This is followed by another swift transition to a dialogue between Cohen and Alex, which contains two surprises for the audience. The first surprise is that Cohen has been prepared to do what Lubin asked, despite the implied insult it carried: he has gone to seek out Alex and find out who he is. We are left to guess at the reason; was it a sense of loyalty to a member of the same firm? The second surprise is that Alex, whom the audience has only seen so far in the role of jazz musician, turns out to be a Primo Levi figure: intellectually a brilliantly gifted mathematician but psychologically in a deeply disturbed state as a result of his period in Auschwitz.

In this small representative section of the play we can see how Vinaver's apparently haphazard approach exposes and clarifies a number of different processes: commercial, psychological, etc. It does this by maintaining its audience's interest simultaneously in a number of different developments. These developments could be listed as follows: (1) the development of the firm's strategy in meeting the American challenge (Will it succeed in coming up with a sufficiently glamorous new product?); (2) the process of marketing a new product (How are such things done? How does a brainstorming session work, etc.?); (3) the development of power relations within the firm (Will Benoit succeed in establishing his authority? Which of the firm's members will make the transition to the new methods?); (4) the development of associated thematic material—(a) power and its relationship to possession(s), (b) conflict and how it may be resolved, (c) pleasure, aesthetic and sensual, and its relationship to trade or exchange; (5) the process of telling a story, writing a play, composing a ballet, and how their different approaches to similar thematic material may intersect or diverge; (6) the development of the love interest (Will Lubin's daughter marry Alex? Will Margerie succeed in gaining control of Olivier's affections?); and (7) the processes of language (How does the choice of language affect a particular encounter? How far is our language consciously chosen, how far imposed by our circumstances? In what ways does our language betray us?).

Linguistic Situations

The last of these, the processes of language, one of Vinaver's abiding concerns, finds its fullest expression in *Par-dessus bord,* a play that exhibits the greatest range of what Barthes called "linguistic situations" (see page 9) in Vinaver's work. The passage analyzed above demonstrates how the language of salespeople, advertisers, consultants, dancers, antique dealers, etc., is never value-free but, rather, carries within it a set of assumptions and tendencies. The excitement of the scenes with Donohue and Frankfurter derives from the skill with which the dramatist makes explicit these tendencies, which normally remain hidden, while making this very process part of the dramatic action. In the early part of the fourth movement, before the section analyzed above, Vinaver presents the first encounter between Benoit (the *Président-Directeur-Général*) and Jenny and Jack (Frankfurter and Donohue, the marketing consultants). This encounter takes place on terrain that is primarily linguistic. Jenny and Jack speak a language that is chatty, uninhibited, unafraid to speak out about intimate things in front of total strangers, unconcerned to respect the normal formulas of polite social discourse. Rather than apologize for being forty-five minutes late, Jack's first words are to blame "your fucking Paris traffic," and Jenny's are to refuse the offered chair, preferring to sit on the floor.

But this apparently carefree and disinterested approach is not what it seems to Benoit. In fact, it is designed deliberately to set up a linguistic situation in which Jenny and Jack will be able to force the bemused Benoit to accept their analysis of his marketing difficulties and, thus, their claim for a large fee. While seeming very casual, they are, in fact, dictating the ground on which the encounter will take place; their free and unorthodox use of language masks a power play through which they are about to establish an irresistible hold over Benoit. They achieve this by shifting the focus of the discourse from intimate human functions to corporate strategies.

> JACK: . . . let me ask you Ben what is it that you sell?
> BENOIT: What is it that I sell?
> JACK: Yes
> BENOIT: Toilet paper
> JACK: What is it used for?
> BENOIT: What is it used for?
> JACK: Yes
> BENOIT: For wiping yourself
> JACK: Wiping what?
> BENOIT: Your behind
> JACK: After you've done what?
> BENOIT: I beg your pardon?
> JACK: After you've done what?
> BENOIT: After you've
> JACK: It's not easy to come out with it huh? It's as hard to get it out of your mouth as it is to shit after weeks of constipation but that's exactly the problem with this joint

JENNY: You're way out of it

JACK: You're selling something that's distant abstract

JENNY: You're not even selling just providing

JACK: Tomorrow if you want to go out there and fight with half a chance of winning you're going to have to sell emotion and pleasure

JENNY: Starting from the act of shitting

JACK: Which is a fundamental human act

JENNY: Enormously rich in emotional repercussions

JACK: And therefore wonderfully suited to the application of marketing

JENNY: Explosive and so far unexploited

(*Par-dessus bord,* 103–4)[6]

Jack and Jenny emerge from this not simply as a couple of rather irritatingly brash American wiz kids, but also as the possessors of a new and powerful language through which the most fundamental realities can be reformulated and structured in such a way as to allow for the application of marketing strategies that will prove hugely profitable. The power struggle that follows within the firm is at least partly a *linguistic* power struggle: the older members of the firm, such as Mme Alvarez, attempt to counter Jack and Jenny's way of formulating the problems by appealing to the "good old values." These are variously expressed as loyalty to tradition in preference to opportunism or as honest-to-goodness strong, reliable paper in preference to the spurious attractions of soft paper, which may feel better but may also disintegrate in your hand. It is because the whole issue is fought out so much on the grounds of language that the brainstorming session provides such a satisfying (and comic) climax. This episode is typical of the play as a whole in that every conflictual situation includes a linguistic dimension, with the result that the play can be seen as a kind of war of different languages: office jargon, marketing jargon, franglais, old-fashioned academic talk, new media slang, jazzmen's "roughtalk," salespeople's smoothtalk, high-finance talk, and many other idioms vie for the right to impose their own construction on the events taking place. In Vinaver's drama of multiple viewpoints no one construction of reality is privileged: the interest and excitement for an audience lies in observing and assessing their rival claims. Even Passemar, the supposed author of the play, finds that his attempts to structure reality are constantly being challenged, particularly by the dancers; this emerges as a witty self-critical comment in which Vinaver recognizes his preference for theater of language rather than the currently fashionable Artaudian "total theater" of the body. Ultimately, he justifies this preference by his brilliantly varied use of language, or, rather, of different languages working contrapuntally. (This contrapuntal technique was to be further refined in the plays of the 1970s and will be discussed in the following chapter.)

With hindsight *Par-dessus bord* can be seen as the play in which Vinaver perfected his play-writing technique. It is the first play in which all the elements he had tried out in earlier works were successfully combined: the dynamics of inclusion versus exclusion, of microcosm versus macrocosm, the intercutting of scenes and interweaving of different time scales and locations, the use of "choral" speaking, the exploitation of different linguistic registers or idioms. It is the first play in which he dispensed with punctuation (apart from question marks), emphasizing the fact that it was not only linear, discursive meanings that he sought to bring out but also ambiguities and poetic resonances. In all of these ways *Par-dessus bord* represents the watershed in Vinaver's career: it contains within it the source of all the subsequent plays that Vinaver was to write in the ensuing decades. In this play he also sets a pattern for his treatment of myth. Just as the different themes, stories, and characters of the play come into collision, fuse, and separate again, achieving effects by juxtaposition, so the play's mythic reference points are drawn from many different sources and are made to interact in unexpected ways. The play contains material drawn from the Norse legends, from Aristophanes, Saint Augustine, Shakespeare, Montaigne, Rabelais, the Marquis de Sade, and Mme de Pompadour, from Freud, Nietzsche, and modern psychoanalysis, from the theories of Max Weber and from the "happenings" of Oldenburg.

But more interesting than the mythical material itself is the variety of uses to which it is put. The dancers, for example, are attempting to use the Norse myths as the basis for new choreography, while Professor Onde attempts to establish the history of the Ases and the Vanes from a purely scholarly perspective. Seeing the transformation of mythic material into modern expressive form in front of their eyes, the audience is led to reflect on other kinds of myth and the uses to which it is put. Through the efforts of a group of jazz musicians to arrange fashionable happenings Vinaver is able to bring in references to *Aktionen* inflicted by the Nazis on Polish Jews: "real happenings," in which excitement was generated through the real blood and suffering of others. In the fundamental struggle between French and American commercial interests each side makes use of the myths that suit it: the French make use of the myth of European culture, and the Americans make use of the myth of American modernity. A similar process is made explicit in the scenes with the antique dealer Topfer, who is able to use the myth of the cultured decadence of the ancient régime to stimulate a collector's passion in the American Margerie. For Topfer the heritage of European culture can be turned into cash value. Similarly, Jack Donohue and Jenny Frankfurter's intervention depends on a manipulation of mythical archetypes: in the first place they rely on the myth of the brash but commercially brilliant American to justify their presence (and their enormous fee). But, more important, their whole sales strategy depends on an appreciation of the mythical associations surrounding defecation: first, they aim to remove the guilt induced by potty training then persuade the customers that a new brand of luxury paper will be the passport to guilt-free anal eroticism. The final choice of "Moss and Heather" is taken because of its ability to encapsulate the myth of cleanliness and release associated with nature.

At another level the play explores the creative problems of the playwright through the figure of Passemar, and it is interesting to see that, rather than create an entirely imaginary character, Vinaver uses his own experience in the construction of Passemar. His first monologue (14–15, largely cut in the abbreviated version) is entirely autobiographical, with the sole difference that the young Vinaver was taken on by Gillette rather than by Ravoire & Dehaze. This use of frankly autobiographical material (the only one in Vinaver's theater) can be explained by the writer's block that he was suffering from in the 1960s. His strategy for overcoming the block was to mythologize his own situation, to allow Passemar to *use* Vinaver in order to explore the various options available to him. In line with this approach Passemar develops as a rather buffoonish figure, constantly losing his grip on his own material. He is portrayed as very much at the mercy of the latest fashions, keen to include whatever is in fashion—nudity, happenings, total theater—yet uncertain as to how to fit all these things into the same play. In the end, like the real author, Passemar decides to borrow his structure from Aristophanes, or, at least, from Aristophanic Comedy as interpreted by Cornford, who maintained that all Aristophanes' Comedies followed a six-part structure consisting of Transgression, Combat, Agon, CounterTransgression, Feast, and Marriage. The six "movements" of *Par-dessus bord* do follow this pattern, and the final words of Passemar ("And thus the end rejoins the beginning") stresses the cyclical nature of the play's subject matter.

In its complete, original version of 255 pages *Par-dessus bord* takes its place in the history of modern drama as the complete Modernist play, worthy to stand beside other "monsters" such as James Joyce's *Ulysses*. It is a work in which all the established conventions and expectations of theater are thrown overboard and the most fundamental principles subjected to self-consciously critical scrutiny. It succeeds better than any other play in the French repertoire in mobilizing conflicting registers of discourse and in showing how their rival claims to explain reality also carry implicit statements about power and control. It tests the old, mythical structures that endeavored to give a unified explanation of the world and finds them wanting but does not therefore reject them, accepting that the twentieth-century worldview must accept the fragmentary awareness of its ruined cultural inheritance. It does not seek to deny the kaleidoscopic fascination of the effervescent cultural life of the 1960s, but neither is it content to stop short at the affirmation of the play of difference. It maintains its affirmation of real human pain and joy, loss and profit, struggling for expression in a world where all the old certainties have been thrown over.

Production History

The production history of *Par-dessus bord* is fraught with difficulties and helps to explain some of Vinaver's hostility toward powerful directors and spectacular, lavish production styles. It was natural for Vinaver to offer the play to Planchon: they had collaborated in the past, and Planchon had, in the intervening years, established himself as France's leading director. The quality that attracted Planchon in the play was its all-encompassing scope; its outsize ambition to represent every aspect of life in Western capitalist society fitted well with his own work as both playwright and director. In *La Mise en pièces du Cid* (1969) he had already attempted to give a global view of French culture and society in the aftermath of the upheavals of 1968; in 1973, the same year that he staged *Par-dessus bord,* he put on a play of his own, *La Langue au chat,* about the state of contemporary Western society and also his second production of Molière's *Tartuffe,* in which he aimed to account for the whole religious and political ideology established during the reign of Louis XIV. But Planchon also had a long-standing fascination with American musical comedy. In *Par-dessus bord* he saw the chance to present the Americanization of

Europe (which is *one* of Vinaver's themes) by borrowing the performance style of the 1940s Broadway musical.

He persuaded Vinaver that his discontinuous structure, with its overlapping time scales, would be impossible to stage; Vinaver agreed to allow Planchon to rewrite the play in a shorter version with a single narrative thread, with added music and dance routines. He argued that this was permissible because of the very accuracy of Vinaver's depiction and that its veracity was such that it would survive an intensely theatrical transposition onto the stage. In the event Planchon's mastery of stage effects was so great that the play was completely drowned beneath the busy surface of glamour, glitz, and visual gags. Planchon had failed to understand the play's fundamental dramaturgical principle, that is, the evocation of a complex reality by juxtaposition of discontinuous fragments. By concentrating everything on a single narrative thread, he turned it into a show resembling one of his own burlesque extravaganzas.

Vinaver's hope that other directors would present the play in different interpretations (as had happened after Planchon's *Les Coréens*) was not fulfilled, although he attempted to make it more accessible by trimming it down to a "brief" version, and even more to a "super-brief" version (the latter is published in *Théâtre I*). The Planchon production was appreciated for its carnavalesque quality, but no other director wished to match himself against this acknowledged master of the stage. Vinaver had to wait ten years for the play's second production (the première of the play as written), which was by Charles Joris, director of the Théâtre Populaire Romand (T.P.R.) at La Chaux-de-Fonds in Switzerland. The Théâtre Populaire Romand had been founded in 1961 as a touring company on the model of the French decentralized theaters of the period. In the course of the company's development its members followed in the footsteps of Copeau, learning from masters of physically expressive theater (drawing on both Eastern and Western sources), devised some of their own productions, but also worked on the classics, including a notable production of Molière's *Les Fourberies de Scapin* in 1982. In May 1983 they moved into a new, purpose-built flexible theater, and Joris made the courageous choice to inaugurate the theater with an uncut production of *Par-dessus bord;* the first night was 3 June 1983. His approach was the reverse of Planchon's. He rejected the frontal performance style and use of complicated stage effects in favor of a multidimensional production in the round with no scenery at all. The performance area was a large open space with a simple framework allowing action to happen on two different levels at once. This framework was used to make it possible for several different scenes to take place simultaneously; seven female and twelve male actors shared all the parts with the help of three musicians. The production was favorably received, and the author had the satisfaction of seeing his dramaturgical experiment at last vindicated in production. In 1991 a major production at the Evora Centre in Portugal by Piere-Etienne Heymann achieved a notable success—see the analysis by Anne Ubersfeld in *Théâtre/Public*, 105.

NOTES

1. Elle semble, au fur et à mesure de sa durée, s'improviser, manifestant une indifférence souveraine pour les enchaînements qu'on pourrait attendre. . . . A aucun moment, ce qui arrive ne devait arriver. C'est l'absolu de l'instant. Non seulement les contradictions et les ruptures de sens y sont constantes, mais constants les décalages de tonalité.

2. *Troilus* devait permettre d'accéder à un théâtre libéré de la fable, ouvert explosivement à tous les possibles, riches de résonances sans limites, informant notre actualité sans nous enfermer dans une leçon.

3. Instrument d'investigation, il a le pouvoir de nous jeter face à des aspects imprévus de nous-mêmes.

4. A partir du moment où il ne s'agit plus de convaincre mais de décrire, les problèmes formels reviennent au premier plan. Car le contenu de la description est inséparable de la façon dont la description est faite. La distinction s'abolit entre forme et fond.

5. Les fétiches nègres que j'adore j'en ai une très jolie collection.

6.   JACK: . . . laissez-moi vous demander Ben qu'est-ce que vous vendez?
        BENOIT: Qu'est-ce que je vends?
        JACK: Oui
        BENOIT: Du papier toilette
        JACK: A quoi est-ce qu'il sert?
        BENOIT: A quoi est-ce qu'il sert?
        JACK: Oui
        BENOIT: A s'essuyer
        JACK: Quoi?
        BENOIT: Le postérieur
        JACK: Après avoir fait quelle chose?
        BENOIT: Comment?
        JACK: Après avoir fait quoi?
        BENOIT: Après avoir
        JACK: C'est difficile à venir hein? Ça fait mal à extraire de la bouche
            comme ça fait mal de chier après des semaines de constipation mais votre
            boîte c'est de ça qu'elle est malade

JENNY: Vous êtes loin loin
JACK: Vous vendez un produit distant abstrait
JENNY: Vous ne vendez pas vous livrez
JACK: Demain si vous voulez vous battre avec une chance de gagner vous allez devoir vendre de l'émotion et du plaisir
JENNY: A partir de ce qui est l'acte de chier
JACK: Qui est un acte humainement fondamental
JENNY: Enormément riche de prolongements affectifs
JACK: Donc merveilleusement propice à l'action du marketing
JENNY: Explosif et encore inexploité

Chapter 4

Chamber Theater

During the 1970s Vinaver wrote four short plays for small casts, two of them published together under the title *Théâtre de chambre (Chamber Theater)*. Like Strindberg, who first coined the term *chamber theater* (in 1907), Vinaver has been a man of extremes, writing either very large-scale works with huge casts or short, intimate pieces with few characters. *La Demande d'emploi* (1971) has a cast of four, *Dissident* (1976) has two, *Nina* (1976) has three, and *Les Travaux et les jours* (1978) has five. All of these plays are written to be staged in the simplest of settings, and all specify that there should be no changes of scene during the performance. The idea of writing small-scale chamber plays occurred to Vinaver while he was struggling with the compositional problems caused by the vastness of *Par-dessus bord;* the first of them, *La Demande d'emploi* was conceived as the obverse of *Par-dessus bord,* taking similar subject matter but treating it in a minimalist style, concentrating on a single dramatic situation. The situation is that of Passemar at the end of *Par-dessus bord.* It depicts a middle-aged businessman named Fage, who has lost his job as a result of the same revolution in marketing methods as the one charted in *Par-dessus bord.*

As in his earlier plays, Vinaver sticks closely to the economic and political realities of the day. After the boom of the 1970s the commercial realities of the 1970s had a very sobering effect on European businesses: austerity programs to reduce government expenditure, rapidly rising costs for industry, the sudden tripling of oil prices in 1973—all these factors led to increased tension in the workplace and made the days of *contestation* in the late 1960s seem suddenly irrelevant. The realities that people faced all too clearly were the struggle for survival in a harsh economic climate and the search for human affection in a divided society.

Vinaver's own professional circumstances also underwent a change during this period, a change that mirrors his dramaturgical shift from the symphonic to the chamber mode. In 1969 he was Gillette's chief negotiator in the firm's successful campaign to acquire control of S. T. Dupont, an old-fashioned family business specializing in luxury goods such as cigarette lighters (also the inventors of the Cricket disposable lighter). In the perception of the Gillette management, there was a major job to be done in bringing this firm into line with modern management and marketing practices. Vinaver was appointed to the post of président-directeur-général and instructed to effect the transition. The location of the firm, at Faverges, a few miles from Annecy, suited Vinaver well, but the job was not a comfortable one. His attempts to rationalize the business met with strong opposition from the work force, which set conditions on the changes and, when these were not accepted, occupied the works. Vinaver himself suffered threats of violence and, because of the relatively small scale of the business, found himself observing at close quarters the human consequences of industrial change. The painful experiences of this decade have nourished all his subsequent play writing. In the plays that follow *La Demande d'emploi* there is less of the Aristophanic humor and the epic, adventurous tone to be found in *Par-dessus bord;* his later plays are more somber (although the humorous effects, especially those generated by irony, do not disappear entirely).

La Demande d'emploi

This is the most experimental of all Vinaver's works; it is almost completely lacking in linear plot structure and is described by its author as a set of exercises for actors. He subtitled the play *"pièce en trente morceaux"* and claimed that "in writing *La Demande d'emploi* I was thinking not so much of writing a play, but of something more pedagogic: a set of exercises for actors. The original title was 'L'Ecole du Théâtre,' and I had in mind the little book of Anna-Magdalena Bach" (*Ecrits sur le théâtre,* 294).[1] The play was, he said, a continuation by other means of the same material dealt with in *Par-dessus bord,* in the same way that Beethoven had followed his Ninth Symphony with the Diabelli variations. Its four characters, on stage all the time, can be likened to a quartet of players, each supplying his or her own characteristic voice or tone. Vinaver has often said that he would rather be a musician or a painter than a wordsmith. In this play he attempted to write dialogue that came as close as possible to musical composition; he called it a "theme and variations" (289).

The theme in question is, like a musical theme, composed of more than one idea. It is described by the author as follows:

> Birth / initiation / transition / acceptance - rejection / self-affirmation - guilt - loss of self-esteem / who I am. (*Ecrits sur le théâtre*, 246)[2]

The nodal experience of the play, through which this theme is developed, is one shared by many of Vinaver's characters: that of "losing one's place"—not only one's place, or job, in a firm, but also one's position in society, one's place in the family and sense of self-esteem. The play's characters are: Fage; Louise, his wife; Nathalie, their daughter; and Wallace, the recruiting director of a specialized travel and holiday firm. The play's thirty "variations" turn chiefly on Fage's experience. The other characters also come in with variations on the main theme, but most of the dialogue centers on Fage.

The musical analogy is helpful in characterizing the special quality of the writing in Vinaver's chamber theater, but it cannot be taken too exactly. Vinaver never aspires to pure abstraction, does not use words solely as patterns of sound, although, like Eliot, he pays as much attention to their sonority and texture as he does to their meaning. Above all, he attempts always to remain faithful to the human experience of reality and to that most fundamental way of relating to the reality around us: telling stories. So all of the characters, whether they are talking about themselves or about others, are constantly sketching out story lines. The author explained this in an interview in 1976 by saying:

> I begin from something which is the opposite of a story. Despite this, I have a need of multiple stories to irrigate the writing, but none of them is allowed to become the main axis, to establish its hegemony. A single story would become a convenient vehicle for meaning. Now for me, today, this vehicle needs to be the juxtaposition of elements that do not fit with one another, in other words, montage. (*Ecrits sur le théâtre*, 290)[3]

So the understanding of reality that emerges for the audience of this play will result not from a central story that "adds up" to an interpretation of the world but, rather, from the sparks of ironic understanding struck when refractory stories or statements or themes are blended together. The word used for this process in Vinaver's notes for the play is *malaxage,* a technical term in chemistry for mixing up substances, which can have the sense of kneading dough or mixing concrete.

This blending process is common to much of Vinaver's work but is taken to its extreme point in *La Demande d'emploi.* In the other plays scenes of blending (like the party sequences in *Par-dessus bord*) alternate with scenes in which the sections of dialogue follow an uninterrupted sequential development. But in *La Demande d'emploi* all the dialogues are intercut with other dialogues, and the writing follows its own associative logic throughout, never the logic of sequential development. This overlapping construction of dialogue is not mere formalistic experiment for experiment's sake. Rather, it is an attempt to find an appropriate dramatic structure for conveying a particular experience of the world. This is where Vinaver's originality lies; he has identified a shift in the way human beings relate to late twentieth-century reality and has struggled to articulate this through the creation of a new dramatic form. The major insight to emerge from all his plays of the 1970s and 1980s is that "the individual may be both crushed by a system and also in perfect communion with it."[4] The cause of this state of affairs lies in the fact that "it is more and more through economics—and not, as was once the case, through the divine—that people weave their link to the world" (*Ecrits sur le théâtre,* 286).[5]

It is worth noting the two rather surprising verbs used by Vinaver in the above quotations: *crush (broyer)* and *weave (tisser).* Both are very characteristic of his way of thinking, and such words recur frequently in his writings on the theater. *Malaxage,* mentioned above, has a similar resonance to *broyer:* both convey a process of pounding and mixing through which human beings are turned into the malleable components of their society; they suggest both the medium and the message, both the disjointed form of the dialogues and the fragmented experience of twentieth-century humanity. Like the words used to convey the sense of being crushed, the verb *tisser,* meaning "to weave," is chosen in order to convey a particular process. In 1976 Vinaver wrote of *Iphigénie Hôtel:* "The action of the play results less from the events than from the totality of the links *woven* by the characters between the events" (*Ecrits sur le théâtre,* 223; my emphasis).[6] If human beings are conscious of being crushed and fragmented by their society, then their only available response is to try to join or knot or weave the fragments together. As always, Vinaver's attention focuses on what is *between* (see page 24); characteristically, he refers to Fage's unemployed state as one of "in-between existence" *(le chômage = un entre-deux)* (246).

Economics, or business, as the medium through which the individual weaves his or her link to the world—but also the system that pulverizes that individual's sense of self-affirmation and of who he or she is—this is the main theme of *La Demande d'emploi.* Each of its thirty variations stresses a different aspect of Fage's economic condition and of its effect on his relationships with others. The dominant factor (joblessness) is always present, but other details are brought in to illuminate this condition from different points of view. Scene 21, for example, might be subtitled "the collector." This is the variation in which the dialogue focuses on Fage's collection of pipes (although there have been several allusions to the collection in earlier scenes). The audience already knows that the collection was started by his father, but it has been inherited and enlarged by Fage. It is presented as a modest attempt to build up something durable to set against the ravages of time: historical objects can give a reassuring sense of continuity to one whose life is in flux, as Margerie found with her collection of eighteenth-century snuff boxes in *Par-dessus bord.*

Scene 21 takes place on Fage's birthday. Louise makes him a present of an antique pipe, a valuable addition to his collection; she has been able to buy it because she has just received her first month's wages. Her presentation speech bears ironic overtones of how a pipe, a collector's item subject to commercial transaction, may be seen to sum up a human tragedy, may even acquire added value from that tragedy.

> LOUISE: Do you like it? It belonged to Captain Bodington, com-
> mander of a ship in admiral Nelson's squadron it has never been
> smoked since the wreck in which he perished
> FAGE: Who?
> LOUISE: Captain Bodington, of course
>
> *(Théâtre I,* 552)[7]

By the end of the scene Nathalie is recounting to her worried mother how Fage has tried to get rid of his collection by going down into the Place Saint-Sulpice and handing out the pipes for nothing to passers-by. This rejection of the basic rules of commercial exchange has aroused the suspicion of the passers-by, who refuse to take them, fearing a practical joke, and of the police, who move him on. Is this episode an indication that

Fage has despaired, is about to commit suicide even? Or does it just mean that he is tired of collecting pipes, sees the absurd side of it? Or is it a gesture of revolt, since the new pipe can be seen as a symbol of Louise's financial independence from him? The collection was his father's: is Fage having a belated oedipal revolt—the memory of his father is raised when he talks of returning to his birthplace, Madagascar? All of these possible interpretations are placed before the audience in the course of the scene.

Other variations present Fage in different perspectives: as father, as husband, depressed, elated, etc. But more often the variations take a notion that can be seen to be ideologically conditioned, such as "responsibility" and then contrasts the different characters' varying perspectives on this notion. Scene 10 could be subtitled "responsibility." It opens with Fage reproaching Nathalie.

> FAGE: You're a sensible girl Nathalie you're not ignorant how could that have happened?
> NATHALIE: What is past doesn't exist
> FATE: But even so this happened
>
> *(Théâtre I, 526)*[8]

This conversation is set in the context of the trip to London, supposedly to arrange an abortion, but where Fage in fact succeeds only in buying Nathalie a sexually provocative dress in the King's Road. The attitude of both father and daughter about how one should face up to responsibilities appears equally inadequate. This dialogue is crosscut with Louise's puzzled questions after their return to Paris and with an episode in the job interview with Wallace in which he is talking of Fage's age and his willpower.

> WALLACE: Your age is not necessarily a handicap
> FAGE: Sport a lot of sport early to bed and enough sleep
> NATHALIE: I want to be able at long last to live without connecting to do one thing completely another thing completely not tying to make links 'cos otherwise
> WALLACE: Sleep yes you want to sleep and you sleep you are a man of willpower you go straight ahead with your jaw thrust out
> LOUISE: And you bought her this dress
> FAGE: You're running away from your responsibilities
> NATHALIE: Responsibilities are obscene

FAGE: It was a special offer
LOUISE: What?
FAGE: Sales
WALLACE: You build your life
FAGE: On the King's Road

(Théâtre I, 527)[9]

This scene shows how the technique of crosscutting dialogues casts an ironic light on statements of value or principle by constantly shifting the perspective. Although Fage may be able to convince Wallace that he is a vigorous person who imposes his will on the world around him, he seems very weak-willed to Louise. He lectures Nathalie on her responsibilities, but his own conduct gives him the lie, and, although members of the audience are unlikely to sympathize with Nathalie's complete rejection of responsibility, they can at least understand why she says what she says. The last two lines illustrate how laughter is generated by this method of crosscutting. Wallace's "You build your life" and Fage's "On the King's Road" are part of two quite separate conversations, but their juxtaposition creates a third meaning, which at first causes laughter because it seems incongruous and then causes a secondary smile of ironic recognition, as the audience sees how Fage's behavior on the King's Road has indeed contributed to shaping his life. Vinaver often uses such reported incidents like musical leitmotifs. Here the report of a significant moment that occurred on the King's Road later finds an echo in the significant action of Fage handing out his pipe collection on the roadside in Paris.

Ironic humor is used by Vinaver in two different ways. One is exemplified by the crosscutting of dialogue just mentioned, pinpointing what the author calls "the equivalent, in writing, of an electric shock, when a current of meaning passes" (*Ecrits sur le théâtre,* 125).[10] The other achieves a less sudden effect by gradually building up the juxtaposition of two apparently unrelated things. In scene 19 Nathalie explains at some length how her lover, Mulawa, is writing a thesis on jokes; as she gives examples of the different jokes he has collected and as Fage goes over the circumstances of his being sacked from his previous firm, the audience begins to see a third meaning emerging: Fage can be seen as not tragic but ridiculous, the butt of barroom stories about bosses who lose their jobs.

As the title of the play suggests, the fundamental dramatic situation enacted in the play is that of the job interview. Everything that occurs in the play is brought to bear, in some way, on Fage's search for employment. Wallace conducts his interview according to what were, at the end of the 1960s, the latest American in-depth methods, probing every corner of Fage's life, however private. It is therefore important for Fage to be able to present his home and family life as blamelessly normal. Scene 15, strategically placed at the center of the play's thirty variations, is exclusively devoted to the interview (the only scene in the play to exclude both women). Vinaver made good use, in this scene, of his professional knowledge of techniques used for selecting staff in business organizations.

Wallace enjoys interviews; he revels in the power to manipulate the applicant and mythologizes his own role, hinting that it has a creative aspect.

> WALLACE: The interviewee to start with is like a field of virgin snow I trace a line a blank canvas
>
> (*Théâtre I*, 532)[11]

More often Wallace adopts a friendly approach, to draw Fage out and encourage him to be open about his attitudes and ambitions. He encourages him to be frank, treats him like an equal. Once or twice he makes a sudden switch to a more aggressive tone, testing how far Fage will allow himself to be pushed without fighting back. The audience is made acutely aware of the self-conscious theatricality of this process. In the course of the scene Wallace repeatedly needles Fage until he finally succeeds in breaching Fage's self-control, provoking an outburst of anger. As soon as he has done this, he stands back and sums up what has just happened.

> WALLACE: Right I note your different reactions ability to take it on the chin self-control reassertion of dignity
>
> (539)[12]

The audience is left wondering whether or not *dignity* is to be understood ironically.

In this interview game Fage has a more difficult role to play than Wallace: he has to decide what it is that Wallace is looking for and then attempt to present himself in such a way that he matches up to it. He has to submit to word association tests designed to reveal his character and to divulge intimate details about his private life. As a result, the audience comes to feel that Fage's whole life is on trial; the quest for work becomes

a quest for self, and Fage's attempt to prove himself worthy of employment becomes an attempt to prove his personal worth or dignity. The
audience shares his anguish but also judges him, as he finds he cannot say
even the simplest things without having the afterthought "How will this
look? What sort of an impression am I making?" For it is clear that Fage
does not entirely dislike being interviewed. The power struggle may be
uneven, but he has at least the satisfaction of being the center of attention.
Ubersfeld provides a detailed analysis of this scene (*Vinaver dramaturge,*
155–60), emphasizing the relentless stripping away of Fage's defenses,
which recalls the technique of Strindberg.

The danger that Vinaver runs in this play is that the action may
become repetitive, since, unlike Strindberg, he does not rely on the linear
buildup of events but, instead, returns with each new variation to the
same central situation. In an interview he explained that by doing this he
was following the logic of the analysis he had made in his article on
Troilus and Cressida:

> We no longer have a body of myth on which one can embroider
> (which was already a form of repetition); we start from zero. Hence
> the importance of repetition, so as to create in the audience's mind
> an initial familiarity with the material, an initial identification. You
> either take a subject that has a good chance of interesting people
> because it has made all the headlines, or you start, like me, from
> what is completely banal, unexceptional. In this case, as soon as you
> have stated it, you have to repeat it. The repetition creates a first
> connivance, ownership, which can lead on to variation, to difference.
> (*Ecrits sur le théâtre,* 290)[13]

In performance what saves the play from the danger of boring its audience
is the frequent incursion of ironic humor and the discontinuities in time.
In order to piece together the fragments with which it is presented the
audience has to construct its own picture of the events as well as to make
value judgments about them. As each new detail emerges, an effect of
suspense is generated, though it is not the traditional suspense of "What
will happen next?" It stems, instead, from the author's use of temporal
discontinuities.

In the first place the crosscutting establishes a particular rhythm or
tempo of interruption: it is constantly leaving themes or stories dangling.
Second, Fage's dramatic situation is closely connected with his experience

of time: he is subject to that particular suspense familiar to anyone who has applied for a job and has had to wait in anguish for the result: at one level a person in this position feels that his or her whole life is in suspense—real time will only begin again when (if) the application is successful. But there is *also* the necessity to fill the time intervening, all the more difficult because of the lack of the routine events that shape one's life in what one thinks of as its normal state. At the same time as living in this suspended state, Fage is obliged to respond to the different rhythms imposed on him by Wallace and by his wife and daughter. Wallace conducts his interview with Fage at a relaxed pace. He makes it quite clear that for him there is no hurry: his priority is the long-term development of the firm and the need to find just the right person who will be able to make the most creative contribution to that development. Louise finds her life developing according to a different rhythm again: that of the mature woman whose child-rearing responsibilities are largely over and who is rediscovering her professional potential. Nathalie is the reverse: she is experiencing the rhythm of pregnancy and is tempted by an anarcho-independent life-style that rejects entirely the career-oriented division of time that has so clearly let her father down.

As Yoland Simon has pointed out, this compositional method creates difficulties for the actor, who has to try to maintain a character *and* show it in different lights, without the help of sequential development through time (*Le Système des oppositions*, 39). Vinaver's only stage direction reads: *"Ils sont en scène sans discontinuer"* ("They are on stage throughout"). The fact that a conversation taking place supposedly in London may intersect with another in Paris, or on a mountainside in the Alps, makes it impossible to present each location separately on stage (unless it were done in the manner of the medieval simultaneous staging). The solution Vinaver had in mind, and the one that has been adopted in every production of the play to date, was to locate the action in a space that would contain elements of all these different locations at once, rather in the manner of a Rauschenberg painting. To stage the play in this abstract space involves work on the actor's voice and position more than on the setting. In fact, as befits a "musical" composition, the space required is more auditory than visual. Vinaver has often spoken of the ideal conditions for the staging of this play as those that allow for *"une écoute attentive* [a sensitive aural appreciation]."

In conclusion, the distinctive quality of the dialogue in this play, a quality that separates Vinaver's chamber theater from the work of other playwrights of the *"quotidien"* school, is best conveyed by the musical analogy with *counterpoint*. This term conveys a compositional technique in which a number of musical lines are set in parallel, each developing according to its own logic so as to create musical effects by juxtaposition. The impression one receives from watching *La Demande d'emploi* is of a number of different dialogues proceeding simultaneously, like so many musical lines, and constantly cutting across one another in such a way as to provoke harmonies or dissonances. In a musical composition such as a string quartet the different instruments can play simultaneously without harming the listener's ability to distinguish each separate melodic line. In a play this is hardly possible, and so, rather than have his characters talking at the same time, Vinaver interrupts one dialogue with a second, returns to the first, continues with a third, etc. Part of the success of this technique, in the theater, derives from the surprise effect of discontinuity when audiences expect continuity. Every time a dialogue is interrupted by another there is potential for the meaning or the emotional tone of one to carry over into the other.

In keeping with the play's discontinuous style and rejection of se-quential development there is no tidying up of ends. The author leaves the audience, however, with enough elements to assemble an ending if they wish. Fage is informed that in the interview process he has come through to the final round, which will be in a few days' time. His daughter takes part in a theft from a luxury shop, is arrested and roughed up by the police—their kicks in her belly may provoke a miscarriage. Louise is promoted. Following his attempt to get rid of his pipes, Fage fails to return home. But none of these events alters the fundamental situation that has been explored in the play. To return to the musical analogy, it is not a resolution but a restatement of the theme that has been explored through-out the play's thirty variations.

Dissident, il va sans dire and *Nina, c'est autre chose*

These two plays, published together as *Théâtre de chambre* in 1978, are constructed on the same principles as *La Demande d'emploi* but are less complex, since they have fewer characters. They are also less experimen-tal in that each tells a story rather than presents variations on a theme. But the method of exploring a human situation used in *La Demande d'emploi* is carried over into these plays, and the story each of them tells is more in the nature of a brief episode from a life than an extended narrative.

Dissident, il va sans dire explores the relationship between a mother and son who live together on their own (the divorced father has moved away). Both characters go through crises in their private lives and in their employment, and each tries to respond to the other's needs in ways that are sometimes clumsy and self-interested, sometimes affectionate and honest. *Nina, c'est autre chose* tells the story of a couple of middle-aged bachelor brothers living together following the death of their mother, from the moment when one of them brings a girlfriend home to the point when she leaves. In *La Demande d'emploi* Vinaver had attempted to write a play whose scenes could be performed in any order, and it is possible to imagine a successful production of that play in which the order is reversed, some scenes are repeated, etc., as is sometimes done with Buchner's unfinished *Woyzeck*. But in these two plays the logic of the development of a dramatic action through an identifiable time span reasserts itself, and the order of the scenes has to be respected.

Dissident is perhaps the most frequently performed of Vinaver's plays and one of the most accessible. It is also his only two-hander. The relationship between mother and son, though intriguing and rich in ambiguities, does not present great difficulties of interpretation, and the character roles are both well within the range of most student actors. The additional advantage of a very simple setting means that the play has become a campus favorite. The dialogue is more typical of the *Théâtre du Quotidien* than that in most of Vinaver's plays: it is halting, inarticulate, emotionally hesitant. It is filled with all the mental bric-a-brac of life in France in the late 1970s: office automation, strikes, the new Renault 5, traffic congestion, etc. This lends the text a surface realism, enhanced by the tendency of both parties, especially the mother, to slip into the standard clichés, telling her son, for example, that he must find himself an aim in life because without that he will never achieve anything worthwhile. With the weariness born of her struggle to be both good mother and breadwinner she attempts to "discipline" him, to improve his manners, to make sure he eats regularly, to instill in him a respect for other people's property. She also tries to be nice to his friends and is hurt when they fail to respond. She has her own problems to cope with, losing her job because of computerization, coping with the death of her own mother, attempting to find a new husband via a dating agency.

Philippe, her son, is in his late teens, unwilling to commit himself to a monotonous job, contemptuous of his successful but absent father, whose attitude to the world remains fundamentally passive; almost despite himself, he is drawn into many different things: drugs, trade union activism, travel. His relationship with his mother veers from the childish to the overprotective, but the main tension between them arises when he fails to communicate or simply vanishes for a time without a word. The play's title suggests the strain of passive nonconformism, which is a feature of so many of Vinaver's young men, and recalls Julien Bême in *L'Objecteur*. It has a double meaning, either a judgmental comment on him or a less loaded descriptive phrase—"Dissident, it goes without saying" or "Dissident, he goes off without a word"—and this ambiguity is indicative of the ironic tensions that irrigate the dialogues between the two. They are incapable of having a straightforward discussion because each is constantly aware of the pressure of the other's expectations. Both are aware of their need for a partner and of the temptation to treat the other as if he/she were that partner, but both also share a strong (though unspoken) awareness of the incest taboo.

The play's twelve scenes chart a development in their relationship, as they work through the variations of parent-child behavior, ending up with a rupture followed by a hint of possible reconciliation. Philippe disappears for a period of weeks, only to reappear when he is already on the run from the police, having become a drug user and having broken into a chemist's shop to steal supplies. Only in the last scene do we see a moment of true communication between mother and son on the basis of mutual acceptance, and this is cut short by the police beating on the door, demanding admission. The movement of the play shows the two characters moving from one stage to another in their mutually dependent relationship. At the beginning this relationship is circumscribed by the normal division of roles between parent as provider and child as object of care and attention. In the course of the action we see both trying out different roles, though they remain dependent on one another, and so each new role involves an attempt to coerce the freedom of the other. At the end, the strains and blocks in their relationship dissolve and they are able to share feelings of genuine love for one another, as if going through all the previous events had been necessary for them to discover one another.

Nina, while similar in structure to *Dissident*, introduces one extra character and reverses the balance of ages and sexes: the two brothers Charles and Sébastien are in their early forties; Nina is twenty-four. Like *Dissident*, it consists of twelve short scenes, with the difference from the other chamber plays that, in this one alone, each scene carries a title. These titles often refer to an object that plays a key role in the scene (e.g., "roast veal with spinach"; "the bathtub"; "the shawl"). Charles and Sébastien are both characters who define themselves primarily in relation to objects. During their lifetimes their overprotective mother had encouraged them to look to her alone for the satisfaction of their emotional needs, and so their life centers on objects rather than on people. Sébastien, the elder of the two, works in a factory, where he is about to be promoted to foreman; Charles is a hair stylist and works in a hairdressing salon.

Eight months before the start of the play the death of their mother has left a gap in their lives, which they have tried to fill by carrying on exactly as they did before: Sébastien takes on the cooking and household management, even learning to cook their mother's favorite dishes, while Charles continues to behave like the indulged baby of the family. Their routine is upset when Charles brings his girlfriend, Nina, back to stay in the house. She challenges their ways of doing things, alternately shocks and charms them. After a while she packs up and leaves the two brothers for a new boyfriend; the last scene shows her returning to visit them. The play's structure is governed by the need to show the transition in the lives of the three characters, as they move from one state to another.

The brothers are well depicted through their dependence on one another, and the way this changes when Charles installs Nina in their flat: he expects his brother to befriend her and encourages her to show him affection, but he is upset when she tries to share her favors equally between them. Both brothers experience a crisis at work; Charles overreacts and turns to alcohol; Sébastien is more stoic. The audience's understanding of what is happening to each character is built up kaleidoscopically, through the juxtaposition of their own accounts and the reactions of the other two characters. The last scene echoes the opening: in both cases we see Sébastien opening a packet of dates, a special present he receives once a year from a girl he knew in Tunisia twenty years before. But in the first scene he is mentally living in the past, whereas by the end he has disposed of the Tunisian memory and is prepared to look to the future. He gives away the dates for Nina to take back to her new lover. For the play to function as the author intended, the third point of the triangle, Nina, needs to be as complex as the other two: she, too, needs to go through a transformation from one state to another. Here Vinaver is not entirely successful; much of the time she appears to serve only to introduce a new element of permissive sexuality into the bachelor ménage. Vinaver fails to show her in the same multidimensional perspective that he achieves for the brothers (or for Hélène and Philippe in *Dissident*), and so the play is weakened by the fact that Nina seems little more than a male sexual fantasy.

It would be easy to mistake these plays, on first reading, for slice-of-life realism; the settings do not change, and the crosscutting is less disruptive to narrative continuity than in *La Demande d'emploi*. But in performance the effect is the same: that of being shown a central situation from a multiplicity of different viewpoints. When these plays have been staged in settings that attempt to build up all the realistic detail of an apartment the dialogue comes across as oddly out of keeping with the setting. This is because the tradition of realism in the theater since the naturalists has taught audiences to look for a dynamic relationship between the characters and the environment in which they are placed. But in Vinaver's work the dynamics are those linking character to character rather than to environment. Naturalism implies a profusion of stage effects: every item on stage is there for a purpose; every object says something about the household or the characters. Vinaver's method, in contrast to this, is minimalist. Although his dialogue may seem to be composed of random fragments of everyday speech, it is, in reality, refined to the point where each line spoken reveals a link between language and ideology. A brief exchange in *Dissident* between mother and son about the pullover he is wearing, for example, reveals two opposed value systems.

HÉLÈNE: Is that a new pullover?
PHILIPPE: Yes
HÉLÈNE: I wonder where the money comes from
PHILIPPE: We pass them around you know
HÉLÈNE: But someone must've bought it

(Théâtre II, 9)[14]

What is important in this sequence is not, as it might be in a naturalist play, the particular kind of garment in question. Rather, it is the whole attitude toward property that is revealed and the sharp contrast that emerges, placing mother and son in opposition to one another.

In *Nina* Sébastien makes a habit of comparing what he imagines to be the different reactions of racial types. When trying to decide what to do with the dates Sébastien says: "Mother used to love them we could send them to help the victims of the disaster in China they put out a press release to say that they were not in need of help from anyone that's what I call pride the Algerians too are a proud people not like the Tunisians what you notice about the Tunisians is their flexibility" (*Théâtre II,* 33).[15] Later in the play he has to make a decision (as foreman) about whether an Algerian should be sacked from the work force at his factory. His habit of racial stereotyping is shown to have an influence on his behavior when it comes to real decisions affecting people's lives. The recognition of this link is not achieved by the building of a causal relationship but, rather, in Vinaver's minimalist style, by suggestion.

It is not always easy for the critic to find the words that accurately identify the difference between Vinaver's method and that of realist (or naturalist) writers. Jean-Pierre Sarrazac expressed the difference as follows:

> On Vinaver's stage most of the remarks are empty, as they often are in real life. Their meaning lies elsewhere: in the gaps, in the dynamic positioning of two sentences, two discourses, two or more characters who are, in themselves, anodyne. In the *montage,* . . . The unusual surface effect is achieved by an extreme economy in the writing: beneath the profusion of the language it is not "outer realism" (and still less "naturalism") that Vinaver is aiming for, but its inner shape, the ideological "lining" of all communication: multiple codes, economic codes, cultural codes, which govern and straitjacket our existence. Vinaver's plays allow us to see, as if in slow motion, or under strobe lighting, as if we could delve deeply into each separate instant, a *linguistic impulse*—one which will conduct an individual "naturally" towards racism, sexism, class collaboration, the sacrifice of sexuality—as well as one which can lead to a gesture of liberation. ("Vers un Théâtre Minimal," 75)[16]

By using the unusual term *ideological lining (doublure idéologique),* Sarrazac is trying to convey the manner in which the ideological implications are not immediately obvious but gradually emerge instead as the hidden underside of the words and actions shown on stage. His use of the words *impulse (poussée)* and *montage* are also striking, because they are words frequently employed by Vinaver himself. He is attempting to show how, through the counterpoint, or montage of linguistic impulses, these plays reveal the ideological implications embedded in the most ordinary episodes of everyday life. The attitudes of Sébastien toward his coworkers in the factory, or those of Charles toward the boss and his employees in the hairdressing salon, reflect just such a montage of linguistic impulses.

Les Travaux et les jours

The title of *Les Travaux et les jours* is borrowed from Hesiod, a writer Vinaver had studied at Wesleyan University and to whom he had returned, first in *L'Objecteur* and then in a long article in *Critique* in 1955. The choice of title was in keeping with Hesiod's theory that the life of a people alternates between periods of epic heroism and periods of quiet consolidation. Vinaver considered that this alternation could be observed in the transition from the 1960s to the 1970s. Like the other chamber plays, it is short (about an hour and a half in performance), concentrated, and has a relatively small cast of five. It is set in a single location, the after-sales office of a firm making coffee grinders, and the characters are the personnel who work in the office: the office manager, Jaudouard; the three telephonists/secretaries who take the calls from the customers and explain how to send a faulty coffee grinder back for repair; and one blue-collar worker named Guillermo, with a workbench, at which he deals with urgent repairs or special cases.

The three secretaries are all women: Anne, who is forty, understands better than the others how the firm works, but her main preoccupation is with her teenage daughter, Judith; Nicole, thirty, has been living with Guillermo for some time, but her life will fall apart when he leaves her; and Yvette, aged twenty, is a newcomer to the office with an eye for the main chance. The three women keep up a constant stream of talk among themselves when they are not on the phone—and often in the middle of phone calls as well—through which they reveal both developments within the firm and the progress of their private lives. They are constantly being harassed, corrected, "controlled" by Jaudouard, the office manager. He is forty-five and experiencing a mid-life crisis. He keeps encouraging them to treat the work of the office as the most important thing in their lives and yet is riddled with doubts about his own usefulness and effectiveness.

In this play Vinaver investigates the ties that bind people to their work and to the other people and the objects in their lives. In speaking of *La Demande d'emploi,* Vinaver pointed out how people construct their links with the world outside them through economics (and no longer through God). He went on to say that the two forces he observed at work in his professional life were, on the one hand, the eagerness to be part of the new economic order and, on the other hand, a terror of being excluded from it. "Comic situations arise from this dialectic in our everyday lives:

we act and think as autonomous producer-consumers, while simultaneously we are consumed, annihilated" (*Ecrits sur le théâtre*, 286).[17] This meditation on the fundamentally commercial nature of all relationships is taken further in *Les Travaux et les jours* than it was in *La Demande d'emploi*. When *Les Travaux et les jours* was written Vinaver had been in charge of S. T. Dupont for seven years. He had been in a position to observe at firsthand the kind of upheavals caused when an old-fashioned family firm is taken over by a large, up-to-date concern such as Gillette. One of the factors he had come up against was the magic attaching to a commercial name that has a long-standing reputation for quality. One might term it, in English usage, "the Rolls Royce factor." S. T. Dupont had just such a reputation, and Vinaver decided to make this *mystique* of the name into a central element of his new play.

For a firm to have built up this mystique the first condition is that its work force must believe in it. The firm of Cosson, in *Les Travaux et les jours,* is one that has a reputation for cosseting its employees. Words such as *faithfulness* and *loyalty to the firm* (words drawn from human relationships) are frequently invoked in the early scenes. Each character in the play participates in this mystique, helps to give it continued validity. The character most prone to this is Guillermo, the repair worker. The reason for his presence in the office is that, when the firm built a new factory in the Vosges some years before, Guillermo had refused to move and so was kept on by this "caring" management out of respect for what he had done for the firm (and his reputation as the best repair worker). He knows by heart the history of the Cosson family and recalls each of the original owners' sons and grandsons. He is also a collector of old Cosson mixers, and nothing gives him greater pleasure than finding one of the original Cosson models at the flea market. Jaudouard contributes to the mystique by his instructions about how to answer requests from customers, explaining to the new secretary that her draft letter of apology to a client might very well pass at Beaumoulin or Mixwell (their competitors) but not at Cosson: "at Cosson we are brief very personalized very attentive and brief" (*Théâtre II,* 64). Nicole, in the opening scene of the play, recounts the story of a caller who refuses to get rid of her Cosson machine because it was given to her by her first husband, who proceeded to throw it at her whenever they had a row. Both she and Anne are convinced that Cosson is a quality firm and that it will look after its employees better than most. Of course, this trust is misplaced, and the action demonstrates the human consequences of these characters investing so much of themselves in the mystique of the firm, how it lays them open to exploitation and lowers their defenses. In Vinaver's own words the play explores the amorous territory that links the business, its employees, and its clients. It is a love story and a love story that ends unhappily.

Vinaver returns to the methods of *Par-dessus bord* in order to dramatize the characters' relationship to their own language: the only language that any of them can speak with perfect fluency is the language of the firm's promotional material. But the more thoroughly they master it, the more of themselves they have invested in it, the more it lets them down in the end. Anne and Nicole, who have both been with the firm for some time, appear to be able to answer the customers' calls automatically, almost without thinking, and they regularly keep two conversations going at once, dealing with the customer on the end of the line without losing the thread of their discussions with one another. The play achieves many humorous ironic effects from the shifts and jumps between the formal terms they use to answer the customers and the intimate tone of their own private discussions. The linguistic registers are so different that at first it seems as though they are able to keep the private and professional aspects of their lives well apart. But, as the play continues, it becomes clear that both have invested their own private emotions in aspects of the firm. In the case of Anne she has built up a kind of familiarity with the firm's managers and their various doings, so that they have become, as it were, part of her own private life. She has taken this emotional investment to the point of having an affair with Jaudouard. Nicole is less fascinated by the gossip of the firm but has allowed herself to become even more deeply involved at the level of her private life, since she and Guillermo are lovers. In the course of the play, as the firm weathers the economic crisis of the 1970s, both of them will be made redundant, and the result of this will be to leave not just their professional lives but also their private lives in tatters.

The only one of the secretaries to come off well is Yvette, who, at the start of the play, is not able to manipulate the correct Cosson formulas at all and has to be taught by the others. But she learns in the course of the play and, unlike her colleagues, is not content to make liaisons with others in the office but flirts with one of the directors in the lift. This turns out to be the right tactic, and at the end she is the only one to be kept on. But the audience is left uncertain about how long it will be before another similar shake up in the firm results in her being disposed of in her turn. For Yvette has had to bear the brunt of Jaudouard's constant sexual harassment of the secretaries in his department. In the office banter that he forces on them seduction of one kind or another is never far from the surface. The power relations that are the "ideological lining" of this sexist banter emerge openly when there are questions of promotion: it is clear that Anne is the person best qualified to take over the running of the office, but it is equally clear that, as a woman and a secretary, she will be denied the promotion. Even a simple request for a partition wall or the right to pin up pictures in the office becomes the subject of a huge trial of strength. Vinaver's dislike of all kinds of hierarchy lends power to his depiction of how these petty tyrannies operate. The only effective resistance available to the secretaries is in expressions of female solidarity: Anne regularly massages Nicole's neck and shoulders, which seize up when she types; Yvette helps Anne with her recalcitrant daughter. But the atmosphere of the office is such that no simple conviviality is possible, and even the friendship between the women can rapidly turn sour, as when Anne becomes terrified that Yvette is gaining an unhealthy influence over her daughter.

In this tense atmosphere each character struggles to find a way of preserving his or her personal integrity. It is easier for the men because, in the unwritten law of the office world, they always dominate. The women expect them to be fairly helpless but at the same time feel obliged to help them to maintain their dominant position. This is part of the way in which they connive in their own exploitation. Each of the men has a particular strength he relies on in order to make up for his other weaknesses or inadequacies. With Guillermo it is the moral strength of his past history, as his father was a fighter for Spanish proletarian rights. With Jaudouard it is the economic strength of his position as office manager, so that he holds the key to the others' chances of promotion. Each of the three women finds herself in competition for the favors of one or both of these men. Both play on the women's good nature, exploit their inbred tendency to want to please, to smooth things over, to help avoid potential confrontations.

In addition to the demands made on them by the internal dynamics of the office they find that further demands are made on their goodwill by the people who ring up. They cannot help noticing that many of the callers are ringing them less because of their broken coffee grinders than because they need to talk to someone. Their natural tendency to respond to such small cries for help is curbed by the firm's demand for productivity improvements and efficiency gains, so that even this limited humanizing of the long-distance communications equipment is cut out.

The pattern of the plot follows the real-life experience of the S. T. Dupont works at Faverges, but it has been manipulated by Vinaver in such a way as to emphasize the theme of the loss of human contact. The company is bought up, economies are discussed, the work force goes on strike. Anne, Nicole, and Yvette cope heroically with the increasing number of calls, calming anxious customers, convincing them that normal service will soon be resumed. But, as soon as a settlement is reached, it transpires that the after-sales service will be the first victim of the economies. Now there will be nobody to talk to the callers; instead, a computer will be installed to send the customer one of a range of sixty-four standard replies drawn up in advance. This is the logical conclusion of a process that the audience has seen at work at a number of key points of the play, when significant events are conveyed through language that is to a greater or lesser extent stiff with specialist jargon, frozen, impenetrable by human emotion. Examples are the memorandum read out by Jaudouard concerning the permitted dimensions of pictures pinned to office walls (*Théâtre II*, 79); the announcement that Cosson will be taken over by Beaumoulin, news that first reaches the secretaries through a newspaper article, in best *Le Monde* economic journalese, which is read out by Anne (85); the printed leaflet circulated by the trade union and which Guillermo is sent with a postscript threatening strikebreakers with violence (95); and the announcement of the reorganization in accordance with the demands of "Logistics" (99).

In such passages the audience is led to reflect on the relationship between the event and the language that is used to mediate that event. As in so many of Vinaver's plays, the effect is of human beings only partly dominating their language; their relationship with language is part and parcel of that larger relationship with the economic system ("both crushed by the system but at the same time in perfect communion with it" [*Ecrits sur le théâtre*, 286]). Their language is like everything else in their world: they struggle to express the emotions and qualities that they wish to affirm, but it turns back on them and crushes their aspirations. This is not only true at the level of the firm but can also be seen in their private lives; Yvette gives an account of an outing on which she has taken Anne's daughter, Judith, including a report of how the daughter does a takeoff of her parents.

She was imitating you Anne and imitating your old man Roger was
doubled up with laughter and me too she gave us a performance of a
speech by her parents Judith you know my darling that what counts
most of all for your father and for me is your happiness true happiness
that you work at not the kind you think you find on the back seat of
a motorbike or in a disco (*Théâtre II*, 101)[18]

Here the dramatic methods first employed in *La Demande d'emploi*
are exploited to the full, since the play explores not one but five different
situations. The dialogues are fragmentary, as in all the chamber theater
plays, mixing up different streams of consciousness and sequences of
ideas. Questions and answers do not correspond; they are interrupted by
other lines of discussion, but through these shifting perspectives five different worlds are built up, each with a point of intersection in the office
but reaching beyond it, too, into the subconscious and emotional worlds
of the characters. The method avoids all the usual traps of melodrama,
sentimentality, and didacticism by this subtle interweaving of themes and
languages. It avoids melodrama by refusing to focus all the dramatic
attention on one story—for example, the story of Nicole, losing first her
lover and her job to the younger girl—but by showing the interdependence
of all the different stories, so that we understand how Nicole's story
cannot be isolated from the takeover of the firm, the experience of Anne,
the struggles of Guillermo, etc. Vinaver controls this complex material
in masterly fashion, and the overall experience for an audience is that of
understanding the interdependence of all the disparate elements in the
play. As Michel Cournot commented after the first production of *Les
Travaux et les jours:* "after a few minutes of acclimatization, the specta-
tor-listener has the feeling that he holds within his grasp the multiple series
of causes and effects contributing to a given event, whereas classic, linear
dialogue reduces these series to a single thread. From this grasp there
arises in the audience a profound emotion, stemming no doubt from the
fact that life itself seems to be captured in the fullness of its flux and all
its mystery" (*Le Monde*, 14 March 1980).

Production History

If Vinaver's intention in writing small-scale chamber plays had been to
avoid the difficulties created for theater companies by the sheer size of
Par-dessus bord, he was successful. Theater people were quick to see

opportunities for performance in these plays, and all of them had been produced more than once by the end of the 1970s. They had become known in the profession partly as a result of the activities of Théâtre Ouvert, founded by Lucien Attoun in 1971. Attoun began by launching a series of staged readings of new plays at the Avignon festival each summer. The readings proved attractive, and he expanded his program to other venues, finally opening a fixed theater at the old Winter Garden in Clichy in 1981. Two of Vinaver's chamber plays, *La Demande d'emploi* and *Les Travaux et les jours,* had their first public showings in the form of Théâtre Ouvert staged readings, and Vinaver's work continued to benefit from Théâtre Ouvert sponsorship into the 1980s, when the first performances of *Les Voisins* were given at the Clichy theater.

La Demande d'emploi was Vinaver's first play since *Les Coréens* to be favored with two different but near simultaneous productions. Jean-Pierre Dougnac, who had been responsible for the staged reading at Avignon in 1972, produced the play at the small Théâtre 347 in Paris in March 1973, and in the same month André Steiger produced it in Switzerland, giving performances at the Théâtre de Carouges in Geneva and the Théâtre des Faux Nez in Lausanne. This was followed by a production at the Comédie de Caen in 1975 by Claude Yersin and further productions in several other *centres dramatiques.* The play's first production received extensive coverage by the drama critics of the French press, all of whom commented on Vinaver's long absence from the stage. Many were complimentary, but Anne Ubersfeld points out that the subject matter provoked responses that polarized along political lines, the establishment papers being hostile, while the liberal press was favorable (see Ubersfeld, *Vinaver dramaturge,* 49–51). This play also provoked the only serious analysis of a single play by Vinaver to have appeared in France: *Le Système des oppositions et le jeu des conflits dans "La Demande d'emploi,"* written by Yoland Simon, a teacher and playwright who works at the Maison de la Culture of Le Havre.

The production of *Dissident, il va sans dire* and *Nina, c'est autre chose* in 1978 was even more successful. It was directed by Jacques Lassalle at the Petit T.E.P. (the studio theater of the Théâtre de l'Est Parisien) and designed by Yannis Kokkos. This time the critics were almost unanimous in their praise, and the production was awarded the Lugné-Poe prize as well as the prize for the best new French play of the season awarded by the Syndicat de la Critique. Again, the plays were quickly taken up by other actors and directors, notably Raymond Braun, who produced them at the Théâtre de Carouges in Geneva in 1980. Lassalle, it was generally agreed, had found just the right rhythm and tempo for Vinaver's texts; he subsequently fulfilled the promise of this production by directing three more plays in the 1980s and 1990s *(A la Renverse, Les Estivants,* and *L'Emission de télévision)*. Not only had Vinaver found, in Lassalle, a director with a real sympathy for his work, but the two plays of *Théâtre de chambre* were also his first to be designed by Yannis Kokkos, whose minimalist style is perfectly suited to Vinaver's writing and who has become a firm friend of the playwright, designing almost all of his subsequent plays.

Les Travaux et les jours provided the first occasion on which Vinaver was able to collaborate with Alain Françon and the company of the Théâtre Eclaté of Annecy, with whom he had been friendly since 1972. In this year the Théâtre Eclaté had produced a play entitled *La Farce de Burgos,* about the trial of sixteen Basques, members of E.T.A., who had been condemned by a military tribunal in Burgos, Spain, two years before. The play was violently anti-Franco and was accompanied by political agitation among trade unionists, especially immigrant Spanish workers. The Centre Culturel in Annecy objected to "political uses of culture" and cut the theater company's grant for the following year. At this point Vinaver provided the company with assistance, writing an article in their support, and making part of his house available to them. After a strenuous campaign mobilizing support the company managed to survive on a project grant and, in the course of the 1970s, built up a strong regional following. In 1978 Lucien Attoun, director of Théâtre Ouvert, invited Alain Françon to produce a staged reading of a new play of his choice in Annecy, and Françon in turn approached Vinaver. At the time he was working on *A la Renverse* but broke it off to write *Les Travaux,* which was given its first staged reading at the Maison des Jeunes et de la Culture in Annecy in March 1979, followed by a full production at Annecy's municipal theater in January 1980 (see *Ecrits sur le théâtre,* 108–10). The reading was attended by some of the workers who had been involved in the factory occupation at Faverges and gave rise to lively discussions about the nature and the uses of political theater. Vinaver himself expressed great satisfaction at the way the play came across in the staged reading and some disappointment at the full production the following year. This experience confirmed his general feeling, developed in the course of the 1970s, that the best productions of his work were the simplest, in which the director's contribution was limited to serving the text, paying special attention to speech rhythms, and adding as little as possible in the way of visual elaboration.

NOTES

1. En vérité, je pensais moins, avec *La Demande d'emploi,* écrire une pièce, que faire quelque chose de didactique, une série d'exercices pour comédiens; le titre à l'origine était *L'Ecole du théâtre,* et je pensais en l'écrivant au petit livre d'Anna Magdalena Bach.

2. Naissance / initiation / passage / acceptation - rejet /affirmation de soi - culpabilité - rejet de soi / qui je suis.

3. Je pars de ce qui est le contraire d'une histoire. J'ai, par contre, besoin d'histoires multiples qui viennent irriguer l'écriture, mais dont aucune n'est autorisée à devenir axe, à devenir hégémonique. L'histoire unique deviendrait le véhicule commode de significations. Or, pour moi, aujourd'hui, le véhicule, c'est la jonction d'éléments réfractaires les uns aux autres, c'est *le montage.*

4. L'Individu peut se trouver à la fois broyé par un système et en complète communion avec lui.

5. C'est de plus en plus par l'économique—et non pas, comme autrefois, par le divin—que les gens tissent leur lien au monde.

6. L'action de la pièce résulte moins des événements eux-mêmes que de l'ensemble des liens que tissent, entre les événements les personnages.

7. LOUISE: Elle te plaît? Elle a appartenu au capitaine Bodington qui commandait un bâtiment de l'escadre de l'amiral Nelson elle n'a jamais été fumée depuis le naufrage où il a péri
FAGE: Qui?
LOUISE: Et bien le capitaine Bodington

8. FAGE: Tu es une fille réfléchie Nathalie tu n'es pas inconsciente comment est-ce que ça a pu arriver?
NATHALIE: Ce qui est passé n'existe pas
FAGE: Mais ça c'est quand-même produit

9. WALLACE: Votre age n'est pas nécessairement un handicap
FAGE: Du sport beaucoup de sport se coucher tôt suffisamment dormir
NATHALIE: Je veux enfin essayer de vivre d'une façon déconnectée on fait une chose pleinement une autre pleinement on n'essaie pas de relier sinon
WALLACE: Dormir oui vous voulez dormir et vous dormez vous êtes un homme volontaire vous allez de l'avant la mâchoire en avant
LOUISE: Et tu lui as acheté cette robe
FAGE: Tu fuis les responsabilités
NATHALIE: La responsabilité c'est obscène
FAGE: C'était une occasion
LOUISE: Comment?
FAGE: Des soldes

WALLACE: Vous construisez votre vie

FAGE: Sur Kings Road

10. L'équivalent dans l'écriture de la décharge électrique. D'un seul coup, ça passe. Qu'est-ce qui passe? Un courant de sens.

11. WALLACE: L'interviewé au départ est comme un champ de neige vierge j'y fais la trace une toile blanche

12. WALLACE: Bien je note vos différentes réactions faculté d'encaisser les coups contrôle de soi sursaut de dignité

13. Il n'y a plus de mythe sur lequel broder (ce qui était déjà une répétition), on part à zéro. D'où l'importance de la répétition, qui crée chex les spectateurs un début de familiarité, donc d'adhésion. Soit on prend un sujet dont on dit qu'il a quelque chance d'intéresser parce qu'il a fait huit colonnes à la une, soit l'on part, comme moi, du banal, du quelconque. Et dans ce cas, dès qu'on l'a énoncé, il faut le répéter. La répétition crée un début de connivence, d'appartenance, qui conduit à la variation, à la différence.

14. HÉLÈNE: C'est un nouveau chandail?

PHILIPPE: Oui

HÉLÈNE: Je me demande d'où vient l'argent

PHILIPPE: On se les refile tu sais

HÉLÈNE: Mais quelqu'un l'a acheté

15. Maman elle les aimait on pourrait les leur envoyer en Chine pour les sinistrés ils ont publié un communiqué où ils font savoir qu'ils n'ont besoin d'aucune aide de nulle part c'est ce que j'appelle de la fierté les Algériens aussi c'est une peuple fier pas comme les Tunisiens chez les Tunisiens ce qui les caractérise ces gens-là c'est la flexibilité.

16. Sur la scène de Vinaver, comme la plupart du temps dans la vie, les répliques sont vaines. Le sens gît ailleurs: dans l'*intervalle,* dans le positionnement dynamique de deux phrases, de deux discours, de deux ou de plusieurs personnages en eux-mêmes anodins. Dans le *montage. . . .* Effet de surface d'une économie sévère: sous la profusion du langage, ce n'est pas le naturel (et encore moins le "naturalisme") que vise Michel Vinaver, mais l'envers, la doublure idéologique de la communication: codes multiples, économiques ou culturels, qui régissent et sclérosent notre existence. Les pièces de Vinaver nous permettent de voir, comme au ralenti, comme sous un éclairage stroboscopique, comme si nous pouvions en sonder les instants, une *poussée de langage,* celle qui achemine "naturellement" un individu au racisme, au sexisme, à la collaboration de classe, au sacrifice de la sexualité, tout comme celle, plus fugitive, qui souligne d'un silence ou d'un spasme un geste pour se libérer.

17. C'est de cette dialectique dans notre quotidien que naissent les situations comiques: nous agissons, pensons en tant que producteurs-consommateurs à part entière; nous sommes simultanément consommés anéantis.

18. Elle t'imitait Anne et elle imitait ton vieux Roger était plié en deux moi aussi elle nous a fait une représcritution du discours des parents Judith tu sais ma petitie chérie que ce qui compte le plus au monde pour ton papa et pour moi c'est ton bonheur le vrai celui qu'on construit pas celui qu'on croit trouver sur le siège arrière des motos dans les discos.

Chapter 5

A Farewell to Sales

At the end of the decade of the 1970s Vinaver withdrew from active employment in the business world and embarked on a new career as full-time writer, teacher, and man of letters. The reasons for this change of life-style were many. In the first place his post as managing director of S. T. Dupont had not brought him satisfaction: the recession of the mid-1970s and its associated labor upheavals had rendered his life at Faverges extremely difficult. On one hand, the logic of his position as managing director trying to ensure the survival of the firm dictated draconian strategies on economic grounds; on the other hand, his sympathies went out to the people who were having to bear the consequences of a painful transition in their own lives. While his working conditions as managing director were becoming less agreeable, attractive opportunities were opening up to him in the field of literature. The productions of his four new plays in the previous decade, together with Vitez's premiere of *Iphigénie Hôtel*, had consolidated his reputation as a major playwright. Moreover, the emergence of the *théâtre du quotidien* had resulted in him being seen as the leader of a vigorous young school of new playwrights (even though his own exploitation of *le quotidien* had its origins in the 1950s).

Bernard Dort and Anne Ubersfeld, two of the senior professors at the Institut d'Etudes Théâtrales (Censier Centre of the University of Paris III), had both been supporters of his work. He was invited to conduct some classes in dramatic analysis in 1983 and then, two years later, to run the first play-writing workshops ever held in a French university. This teaching activity proved so congenial to him that he allowed it to take up more and more of his time, becoming a titular professor at Paris VIII (St. Denis) in 1988. In addition, he played an active role in the organization of the

Centre National des Lettres, chairing its first theater panel and conducting an extensive survey on the reasons for the disastrous collapse of dramatic publishing in France in the course of the 1970s. The text of this survey was published by Actes Sud in 1987 as *Le Compte rendu d'Avignon,* reflecting the fact that Vinaver's first presentation of his findings had been made at the Avignon Festival in the previous summer. Its subtitle (an ironic reference to the popularity of long, pretentious titles) was *"Des mille maux dont souffre l'édition théâtrale et des trente-sept remèdes pour l'en soulager."*

The 1980s thus saw Vinaver turning away from business and involving himself in activities that are more common for a writer in France, but not before he had made his farewell to the commercial horrors of the 1970s by writing *A la Renverse.* This was completed in 1979 and was seen in a production by Jacques Lassalle at the Chaillot theater in 1980. At the level of subject matter this play marks a return to the areas explored in *Par-dessus bord:* it deals with eight months in the life of a firm manufacturing suntan cream. It shows how this firm is bought up by an American conglomerate, squeezed for maximum profit, and then sacrificed when it runs into difficulties. Vinaver drew on firsthand experience at Gillette and S. T. Dupont in order to depict the workings of the commercial world with his usual insight, and the territory in which the play is set is very similar to that of *Par-dessus bord.* But the underlying aim and direction of the play are in fact quite different. Vinaver expressed the difference by saying that the first play was written in the epic phase of French capitalism, whereas in *A la Renverse* something has begun to go wrong in the system: "We have moved from Homer to Hesiod: there is nostalgia and a sense of cracks opening up" ("La Banalité dans le désordre," 7).[1] In *Par-dessus bord* the purpose was to explore the interaction between the commercial system and the human lives that gave it its lifeblood but also found themselves devoured by it. In order to be true to the multiplicity of activity and experience involved in such a project Vinaver had been obliged to write a gigantic play involving a mammoth cast and extending over a long period of time. In *A la Renverse* the central character is the firm itself; there is far less attempt to explore the individual human realities out of which the firm is composed. Instead, the plot is streamlined in such a way as to emphasize the changing fortunes of the firm itself, as corporate body, and to minimize the particular individualities of the human beings involved.

The stage directions consist of an unusually detailed description of the *dispositif scénique*. This specifies a central acting area that is bare, apart from some typical office/boardroom furniture; on this central space all the events of the play are acted out by a cast of six actors who represent, between them, about two dozen different characters; on the fringes of this area there are to be three *espaces-satellites,* or ancillary spaces, each with a separate population and furnishings molded in white plaster. The first of these secondary spaces represents the boardroom of the Sideral Corporation of Cincinnati, with the five members of the executive committee all molded in white plaster. The second space represents a French family of four sitting around their dining table and watching television while they eat. In this space the family group's clothes, as well as themselves and their furniture, are molded in white plaster. The television, however, is real and operational; the program that is being watched will also be seen by the audience in the theater, as it is relayed on monitors placed around the auditorium so that every member of the audience is within easy viewing distance of a set. The third space represents the workshop in the plant where the bottles and tubes are filled with the cream; it contains a real machine, working, and three female workers molded in white plaster. Vinaver notes that each "satellite" has its own soundtrack, meaning that where there is dialogue between the characters this should be done in "voice-over." He also makes use of the device of a prologue and epilogue in voice-over, by which means the story is introduced and concluded.

The play is grounded, according to its author, in the musical structure of the prelude and fugue, the prelude taking the first twenty-eight of the play's one hundred pages in the version printed in *Théâtre II* (111–38). In choosing this structure, he had in mind something rather different from the theme-and-variations structure that he had used in earlier plays of the 1970s. That structure had allowed him to explore the multiple ramifications of a particular idea or event on a limited number of interpersonal relationships. In *A la Renverse* the characters are treated entirely differently. Vinaver himself explained that "in *Par-dessus bord* the characters had an identity from start to finish. In *A la Renverse* they have no contours. The attempt is rather to show numerous characters (played by six actors) fading away" ("La Banalité," 7).[2] Here the raw material is not the life of the characters but that of the firm. Large parts of the play are written in the form of dialogue without specific attribution to speakers, so that many of the lines might be spoken by any one of the six actors. The method is similar to that employed for the "party" sequences in

Par-dessus bord and creates the impression of the existence of a corporate body in which the individuals lose their separate identities. Vinaver's notes to the play insist that the actors must avoid "any temptation to interiorize" (*Ecrits sur le théâtre*, 263). He does so because the private lives of the people who make up the firm have to be seen to fade into the background. Where speakers *are* identified by name in the text the action is concerned with decisions being debated or taken that will affect the life of the company: they involve union representatives or managers (known in French by the impersonal term *cadres*).

So the different themes that are stated in the prelude and then worked into the fugue are abstract in the sense that they represent generalized group attitudes. They can best be expressed in terms of the aspirations of each particular interest group within the firm. The union wants job security and some control over management decisions; the sales staff wants a product they can believe in and a good sales pitch so that they can persuade the retailers to take it on; the managers want to maximize profits so as to satisfy the American owners. As for the board in Cincinnati, they are only interested in the firm's balance sheet. The play shows these different attitudes being expressed, first one after the other and then in counterpoint, exactly as they would be if they were musical themes in a fugue. As they come into conflict with one another, the incompatibility of the different segments of the firm is demonstrated, and a classic Marxist analysis of alienation in the workplace is built up, as the audience sees how the interests of the American owners are opposed to those of the French work force. There are additional refinements to this classic presentation, as the founder of the American holding company finds himself fired by his own board and the most inspired member of the sales force finds himself blocked by conservative management thinking.

The style of the writing is reminiscent of oratorio: it consists of choral passages in which different groups confront one another and voice their collective views. It contains very little dramatic action, since there is little scope for any of the groups to make a positive move. Most of the time they are placed in the position of reacting to events over which they have no control. The story starts with an old-style French family firm, Les Laboratoires du Docteur Sens, marketing various ointments under the label Les Pommades du Docteur Sens. In the late 1960s the aging Philippe Sens takes on Aubertin, an energetic young graduate of the *Hautes Etudes Commerciales* (HEC) who transforms the firm by streamlining its operations and selling to an American conglomerate: Sideral of Cincinnati. The result is massive new investment in the production of suntan cream and a change of name to Bronzex. Aubertin succeeds in head-hunting an outstanding salesman from Ambre Solaire, who names the new product Mi Fa Sol, and the result is a huge success, providing the firm with rapid growth and fat profits. This much is set out in the voice-over prologue. When the action begins the firm is about to launch its successor to Mi Fa Sol, and the management is torn about whether to continue the musical analogy by calling it Si Do Ré or to opt for the more evocative name Corps Libre. But a new element has entered the field: a society lady—La Princesse Bénédicte de Bourbon-Beaugency—who is dying of cancer, has agreed to do a television series, in which she will appear for half an hour every Saturday evening on "Antenne Deux" to discuss her progress toward death. The cancer from which she suffers began with a melanoma on the temple and can be positively attributed to the effect of excessive exposure to the sun.

This television series captures the imagination of the whole nation, and the result is a sudden collapse of the market for suntan cream. At first the Americans think that this is no bad thing: it will sort out the market so that, when the sunbathing fashion returns, Bronzex will have the whole field to itself. But the rejection of sunbathing proves more widespread than expected, and Sideral insists on the firm's work force of eight hundred being reduced to three hundred. The company also replaces the energetic Aubertin with an accountant, Claisse. The workers occupy the plant and refuse to accept the decisions handed down from Cincinnati. After toying with the idea of diversifying into other leisure products, the Americans decide that the simplest thing is to cut their losses and sell the business for the symbolic price of one franc. Their initial investment has been recovered many times over, and it is more advantageous for them to sell than to allow one of their affiliates to go bankrupt, rendering them liable to pay its debts. The workers' occupation forms itself into a cooperative and buys the business, taking the company's former name again. An afterword informs us that they survive, but only just, because the fashion has turned definitively against sunbathing. In the meantime Sideral has made some disastrous investments, and its shares collapse, only to be bought up by Siderman, the original entrepreneur and owner, who, after being sacked by his own board, has formed a new company exploiting solar energy and has built it up to the point where he can once again travel the world looking for investment opportunities. He has made a date to come and cast his eye, once again, over Les Laboratoires du Docteur Sens.

Many of Vinaver's plays could be said to be about the workings of capitalism, but this is the only one that takes the capitalist process as its exclusive subject. It presents capitalism as a dynamic, self-perpetuating system that can turn its own defeat into the principle of a new advance and recalls Sartre's analysis of the ship-building business in *Altona,* with its theme of *qui perd gagne* (loser wins): "The play envisages capitalism as a reversible engine. Every catastrophe propels it forward" ("La Banalité, 8).[3] The success or failure of individual products or firms cannot damage it. Capital will flow, rapidly and flexibly, to whatever new commercial opportunities present themselves and will even be able to feed off the corpses of enterprises that have collapsed. This is the reality of the commercial world dominated as it is by multinational conglomerates that are sufficiently diversified to be able to play off one business interest against others.

The emphasis in Vinaver's dramatization is on how the various groups are always somehow out of step with reality, unable to grasp the economic demands of the situation, whose contours are elusive, changing faster than they can be understood. Vinaver called the play an "economy fiction," and the general atmosphere of the play recalls that of Borges's *Ficciones* (much admired by Vinaver). Borges's story "The Lottery in Babylon" imagines the affairs and government of Babylon entirely determined by a mysterious company whose function is to run the national lottery. The total control acquired by this company is attributed to a breakthrough at an early point in its history, when it was realized that the appeal of the lottery would be greatly enhanced by including penalties as well as prizes. There was a great popular movement demanding that everyone be able to take part in the lottery on an equal basis. As a result, participation became a universal right. "The consequences were incalculable. A fortunate play could bring about promotion to the council of wise men or the imprisonment of an enemy. . . . A bad play: mutilation, different kinds of infamy, death" (Borges, *Labyrinths,* 32–33). The draw became inordinately complex, every prize or penalty depending on the accumulated results of an enormous number of draws, and so, in order to protect itself, the company had to operate in secret. After many years the Babylonians came to doubt whether there even existed such a thing as the company "because Babylon is nothing else than an infinite game of chance" (35). Vinaver's depiction of the workings of the capitalist system has something in common with Borges's Babylonian lottery. The winners and losers of *A la Renverse* seem to emerge in as haphazard a manner as if everything were governed by the laws of chance, and, although the analysis of the conflicting class interests follows an orthodox Marxist line, the play carries no implication that the logic of the historical dialectic will lead toward a proletarian revolution. Instead, it puts the emphasis on the unexpected, illogical twists of history: the events that may seem most significant from a Socialist perspective (such as the successful occupation of the factory) are more than likely to be neutralized by an unforeseen development in the global economic context.

By dramatizing his material in this way, Vinaver ran the risk of presenting only the banalities of the firm's life, without including the element that enlivened his other plays: the investigation of how people live with these things, constructing their lives by and through them. As a sort of counterweight, he introduced the sequences in which the princess gives a detailed account of the progress of her illness and of her attitude toward her approaching death. These sequences are all in the form of television interviews, with the interviewer off-screen, and some scope for the director to create an appropriate video-film. In the first production Jacques Lassalle handed over direction of the film to Jean-André Fieschi, a film critic and director of some distinction. Bénédicte was played by Emmanuelle Riva, who gave a performance of great power and authenticity, filmed in sumptuous interiors, suggesting a royal chateau. In performance these filmed sequences stole the show. Here was a story with which every member of the audience could identify—a story that, unlike the rest of the play, focused on one individual and followed her development. This was a blow to Vinaver, since he had aimed, in writing these sequences, to avoid such audience identification. The princess reveals herself, through the things she says, as a superficial, sentimental, and profoundly silly representative of her class. Moreover, the interviewer's comments clearly reveal his voyeuristic delight in having persuaded her to make a spectacle of her death, never failing to remind his audience of the fact that they are in the presence of a woman irremediably condemned to die and hypocritically attempting to assume a tone of sorrow when he can hardly conceal his delight at the program's massive ratings. On the page the scenes are profoundly comic. But in performance the pathos of Bénédicte's situation carried all before it: Vinaver had understood only too well the power that such a series of broadcasts might have but had not been able to prevent his real audience from succumbing to it.

It is notoriously difficult to mix the media of television and live drama in the same performance. When Vinaver returned to the subject of television a decade later with *L'Emission de télévision* he did not make the same mistake again. *A la Renverse* represents a first attempt on his part to try to investigate, by dramatic means, the power of the media in modern France. It is partially successful in showing the power of the mass media and how they may have effects that are quite out of proportion to the importance of what they show. His experience in commerce had shown him what a powerful medium for propaganda the television can be, whether it is deliberately promoting a product or making claims to objectivity. But his model of how television has this effect was too simple. The development of his plot depends on the assumption that a series of broadcasts like those of Princess Bénédicte could have the effect of completely eradicating the fashion for sunbathing. History has proved him wrong, since despite well-publicized skin cancer scares, the 1980s did not see the end of sunbathing. On the contrary, the pharmaceutical firms managed to turn the fears of sunbathers to their own commercial advantage by marketing skin creams that claimed to block out ever more of the sun's rays, thus enabling holidaymakers to enjoy the pleasures of exposure to the sun without suffering from its dangerous effects (or so they claimed).

Vinaver's failure in this respect is odd, since an early sequence in the play explains very convincingly the profound psychological impulse that lies behind the sunbathing habit. This sequence shows that the emotions of the sunbather are not simply those of pleasurable relaxation. At one level, of course, the experience is satisfying because of the sensations of warmth and relaxation, but beyond that it can also have associations of a more disturbing nature. It may be seen, for example, as a kind of sexual self-giving, as in D. H. Lawrence's story "Sun," in which the heroine feels "a desire to go naked to the sun" and, when she does so, feels the "conviction that the sun was gradually penetrating her to know her in the cosmic carnal sense of the word" (116–42). At an early point in the play Vinaver includes a sequence in which one of the executives reports on the results of an inquiry into the motivation of sunbathers: "The act of going brown means allowing oneself to be penetrated . . . solar penetration being diffuse induces a pleasure that is less climactic but equally gratifying especially since it entails no guilt feelings" (*Théâtre II,* 124).[4] Added to this is the semipantheistic pleasure of feeling at one with nature, but even more important is the small dosage of fear accompanying it: "It should be noted that any pleasure is intensified by being mixed with its complementary opposite, i.e., fear" (125).[5] Vinaver here placed in the mouth of one of his characters the very element that was, in reality, to ensure that sunbathing has not lost its popularity, despite the fear of cancer. Sun worshippers have not been put off by the discovery that their god is a savage god; if anything, the discovery has increased the god's appeal. But Vinaver failed to draw the correct conclusion for the development of the action of *A la Renverse,* and so the play suffers from an underlying inauthenticity.

In the case of some dramatists this might not be a serious charge, but in Vinaver's case it matters, since his aim is to create his dramas from the authentic magma of everyday life. Part of the success of *Par-dessus bord* can be attributed to the fact that the play was true to the upheavals convulsing French industry at the end of the 1960s; in fact, a take-over battle was fought for a toilet paper manufacturer shortly after Vinaver had finished *Par-dessus bord,* in which the broad outline of Vinaver's plot was followed almost to the last detail. In *A la Renverse* he failed to use his understanding of the psychological drive behind the commercial product to foresee the way in which the market would in fact behave. There is an added irony in his failure to do this, since the events of the 1980s have served to make his central point rather better than he did: the pharmaceutical industry's real ability to overcome the fear of cancer demonstrates even more clearly than Vinaver's play how capitalism is able to digest elements apparently hostile to it, turning them to its own advantage.

The production of *A la Renverse* met with an unusually hostile reaction from the critics, despite the quality of Fieschi's video-film, Kokkos's sets, and Lassalle's direction of some fine actors. The play was accused of failing to rise above the level of cliché and platitude. Such reactions are understandable in light of the difference between this and Vinaver's other plays set in the world of commerce. The experience of *A la Renverse* suggests that Vinaver is right to say that he needs to start from a principle of nonselectivity; only in this way can his dramatic material convey the sense of complexity or multiplicity that can illuminate what would otherwise be a very ordinary situation. In his notes Vinaver states: "The business = total living environment" (*L'entreprise = total lieu de vie*) (*Ecrits sur le théâtre,* 262). But the firm of Bronzex never achieves this kind of totality (unlike the firm of Ravoire & Dehaze in *Par-dessus bord* or the firm of Housies in *L'Ordinaire*). There is a contradiction apparent in the stated aim of presenting the business as a total living space and that of selecting only those events relevant to the development of the firm. An audience is left without very much human response to the sterile living environment of Bronzex. Vinaver seems not fully to have grasped this contradiction at the time of writing the play, since he comments in his notes on "the couple Bénédicte-Pellepain: two 'heroines,' each occupying one of the two hemispheres of the popular dreamworld—figures of woman—the princess (tragic) and the shepherdess (epic)" (264).[6] But, by adopting a predominantly choral method in his writing, he made it impossible for Mireille Pellepain to emerge with the same force as Bénédicte. Apart from the brief hint of a developing relationship with Piau at the end of the play, Pellepain never appears in any role other than that of spokeswoman for the union, whereas Bénédicte always appears alone and is urged by the interviewer to reveal all the different aspects of her life, both public and private. There is thus a radical imbalance between the ways in which the two characters are presented to the audience, and the two characters fail to emerge as occupying contrasted roles in the popular imagination.

L'Ordinaire

After the abstract fugal style of *A la Renverse*, *L'Ordinaire* returns un-equivocally to the drama of closely observed individuals. It opens on a discussion between two ex-lovers and develops, in the course of the plot, a complicated network of personal and sexual rivalries between its nine major characters. Its plot is strictly linear, telling a story of survival that makes use of traditional suspense. The characters in the play all relate in some way to the construction company Housies, specializing in the pro-duction of cheap, prefabricated housing. Bob, the company president, and his three senior vice presidents—Ed, Dick, and Jack—are on a tour of South America, the purpose of which is to acquire a franchise from the governments of Brazil, Argentina, Chile, etc., to install production lines for the manufacture of Housies and thus solve the "problem" of the shanty towns around the major cities of the continent. Traveling with them are Joe di Santo,the company vice president in charge of Latin America, and his eighteen-year-old daughter, Nan. Jack has brought along his mistress, Sue, and Bob is accompanied by Bess, his wife, and Pat, his secretary. The cast is completed by the pilot and copilot of the company jet in which they are all traveling. Crossing the Andes en route for an interview with General Pinochet, the plane is caught in exceptionally bad weather and crashes into a snowfield on the side of a mountain. Both the pilots and Joe di Santo are killed in the crash; Pat the secretary has her legs badly crushed. The major part of the action follows the survival of the eight remaining characters as, one by one, they die, leaving in the end only Sue and Ed.

The situation is one of the most concentrated and intense of any of Vinaver's plays and can be understood on a number of different levels. In the first place it is an exciting story of survival after a disaster. Vinaver employs all the traditional elements of such stories: the suspense of the dwindling rations; the rivalry between different people's ideas of how to escape; the despair when rescue planes can be seen but fail to spot the survivors; the expeditions that set out to attempt to find a way down the mountain; the avalanche that kills off all but the last two of the party. The crash takes place halfway through the first scene, and the remaining six scenes are spread out over a period of forty-two days. The survivors only manage to stay alive for this length of time by resorting to cannibalism, eating the flesh of their dead companions, which, because of the intense cold, remains perfectly preserved. This is the second level at which the play may be read: as a play about social taboos and how they may, in extreme circumstances, be breached. The means by which the taboo is broken and the stages through which the group's cannibalism develops form a fascinating study in social dynamics. As usual, the playwright remains strictly within the bounds of verifiable fact and contemporary event: the story was partly based on that of the Uruguayan football team, which crashed in similar circumstances and survived by the same means until rescue came. In newspaper interviews after their rescue they explained that they had been able to overcome their natural revulsion at the act of eating human flesh by treating it sacramentally as the body of Christ, a psychological mechanism that Vinaver, too, builds into the action of his plot.

A third level of meaning to be found in the play is its examination of the group dynamics at work in the management team of a large American industrial concern. In this case the interest is twofold—not only that of understanding how decisions are reached but also that of seeing how characters who have been successful in this world develop (or fail to do so) under the pressure of the unexpected. The common currency of management techniques, such as the need to be "proactive" rather than "reactive," is subjected to severe testing by the strict limitations of the situation into which the whole management team is thrown. By his use of the contrast between "ordinary" ways of doing things and the extraordinary situation they are now in (whose problems are, however, the strictly ordinary ones of finding the food and warmth necessary for survival)

Vinaver develops an ironic commentary on the workings of business in the industrialized nations. From this there emerges yet another level of meaning: a mythological or poetic meaning. For, while the incidents of the play remain realistically rooted to the microcosm of the mountainside in the Andes, the situation of these cannibal industrialists acquires a macrocosmic resonance, conveying the whole relationship between the "First" and "Third" worlds and the mindset that characterizes the leaders of Western industry.

The play opens in the cabin of the Housies jet; Bob, Bess, Dick, and Joe are playing cards at a table; Pat, the secretary, is typing a letter; the others are sitting or lying down. Sue speaks the opening line: "C'est fini Jack" (It's finished Jack). This, combined with the restricted space and the portholes out of which the characters peer from time to time, suggest a reference to Beckett's *Endgame,* and in fact Bob, seated at the center, indulges in behavior very reminiscent of Beckett's Hamm. But the setting in which this "endgame" will be played is quite different from Beckett's nonspecific environment, and the first scene serves the traditional expository role of building up a picture of the world these characters inhabit. Sue and Jack are arguing about the end of their affair; Sue has begged a lift in the Housies jet because she wants to start again from scratch in Santiago. Jack is trying to protect her, despite her decision to put him off, and insists that she'd at least have a better time in Rio. Beginning as the most marginal figure of the whole group, Sue will gradually reveal herself as the undisputed leader and the person best able to adapt to the new circumstances forced on them all by the crash.

Immediately following the short dialogue between Sue and Jack comes another between Pat and Ed, which serves to show that the night before, at the Excelsior Hotel in Buenos Aires, they shared the same bed for the first time. Then the focus of attention switches to Bob, the president, who is throwing his weight about, calling for the copilot to bring more drinks and exulting in the ease with which business deals can be pushed through in South America by contrast with the difficulties of operating in Europe. Bob is rapidly established as the authoritarian center of this group and the "matey" use of monosyllabic Christian names as a mere pretense at equality. Bob expects those around him to massage his ego or to supply a service that he needs and cannot supply himself. His outward show of conviviality is completely divorced from his brutal attitude toward others involved in the running of the business. This emerges amusingly (for the audience) as he dictates a letter to the Buenos Aires branch manager, in which he criticizes his work, makes it clear he is to be dismissed, but finishes with affectionate personal greetings to him and his wife, as if nothing were amiss. As the weather conditions deteriorate and the pilots express their anxiety, Bob begins a rambling review of his managers in various cities around the globe with a view to finding a replacement for Buenos Aires. Bob continues to play his power games, oblivious to the external conditions, but the audience sees all too clearly that the plane is about to crash, and in this way the fundamental ironic contrast of the play is established: it is the contrast between Bob's delusion of controlling the world and his real position as the helpless plaything of wind and weather.

The crash is conveyed economically by the stage directions *"bruit, noir,"* followed by the projection onto a screen of a telexed press release. The lights then come up to reveal the mountainside with the broken fuselage of the plane half-buried in snow. Eight days have passed, and the survivors have begun to establish a modus vivendi. Bob's need to be seen to be in control is instantly reinforced for the audience, as he obsessively reckons up the inventory of the plane's dwindling store of food. The group's initial certainty of being rescued is beginning to fade: on the radio a newscaster announces that the Chilean authorities have called off the air search. Nan and Jack have gone off to try to locate the body of Nan's father, thrown from the plane when it broke up, a few seconds before coming to land in the snowfield. They return, having found him, and, amid the lamentations of Pat for her crushed legs (*"Mes jambes c'est ce que j'avais de mieux"* [My legs were my best point]) and of Dick, who is in agony from a piece of metal protruding from his stomach, the question of feeding on human flesh is broached for the first time. The manner in which the subject is broached is instructive in view of subsequent developments: the mention and discussion of the subject is confined to the women. The first tentative suggestion comes from Pat: the secretary is the one who always has to find practical solutions to problems that defeat everyone else. She is quickly silenced by the rather pious Bess, who tries to suggest that her injuries have made her hysterical. The men make no direct comment, but Jack and Dick start to have a furious row about their exact position and the best way to climb out. Finally, it is Nan, Joe's daughter, who provides the permission that is crucial to lifting the taboo by saying:

Mister Lamb I am sure that daddy would agree if he knew that all
we have left is a few olives and some crackers
He would agree with what Pat said.

(Théâtre II, 314)[7]

A few moments earlier Bess had summoned up the courage to extract the
piece of metal from Dick's stomach, and from this point onward it is
essentially the women who demonstrate the courage and inventiveness
necessary to survival on the mountainside, while the men appear, to a
greater or lesser extent, to be locked in the hierarchical patterns of the
Housies power structure. In this way a reversal of power operates, as the
women, who were all marginal to the male-constituted power structure
before the crash, take over the initiative.

It is not until scene 2, three days later, that they finally reach the point
of eating human flesh for the first time. The scene starts with Bob rehearsing his heroic struggle to reach the summit of his business career. Vinaver
opens up a grotesque contrast between his boasting attitude toward the
others and his real situation, marooned at the summit of a mountain range
on this continent that he treats with a combination of scorn and sentimentality. He then starts to arrange for the departure of an "expeditionary
force," but it is evident to all that they are too weak and have almost no
food left at all. Sue reveals that she has cut up the body of one of the
pilots and spread some strips of meat on the fuselage to dry in the sun and
urges the others to eat. Bess is, once again, deeply shocked and resorts
to accusations that Sue has an evil influence over the whole party, remind-
ing them that she had no official business to be on board in the first place.
Finally, she, Jack, and Ed begin to eat; Nan can only vomit but declares
her intention to eat as soon as she can. Bob, Bess, and Dick watch them,
and, while the first tentative mouthfuls are being taken, Bob raves on
uncontrollably about how to manage his business associates, while Bess
insists that they are offending god and will be punished for it.

The strength of the scene lies in its counterpoint of contrasting attitudes, which succeeds in short-circuiting normal reactions or defense
mechanisms, thus presenting everything that happens in a new light. The
scene achieves a shock effect but does so by emphasizing the ordinariness
of the act, not by dwelling on its horror. Sue's attempts to persuade the
others to eat are met with complicated evasion tactics by Pat, who is too
ill to think clearly, and by Bob, who instinctively reacts against anyone
else taking a leading role. Pat talks feverishly of her Young Divorcees'

Club, which is about to have its Annual General Meeting (AGM) and for which she has had to write a report. Her concerns are clearly of minor importance according to the normal hierarchies, but on this terrifying mountain, facing death, there is something heroic about her concern—as Sue says: "Vous avez une existence débordante Pat" (You have a very full life Pat). The discourse of Bob, reviewing in his mind the staff he means to sack or move around, would undoubtedly have a damaging effect on a great many lives if he were in his office at Seattle; here on the mountainside it seems completely gratuitous, with no purchase on reality. Life is on the side of those who eat—those are the plain, "ordinary" conditions in which they find themselves.

Scene 3 takes place five days later. Pat has died from gangrene; Jack is trying to get the radio to work; Dick supports Bob in his conviction that Reagan will send a team to rescue them. Bess has reconciled herself to eating the flesh of the dead members of the party by treating it as if it were the Sacrament. The radio announces that a couple of American search planes have indeed been sent out to Chile but that there are also reports of a left-wing guerrilla band hoping to make hostages of the party. Dick and Jack quarrel violently; everyone expresses their private anxieties about what the guerrillas might do to them. Finally, Bob dominates the end of the scene with a rhapsodic rehearsal of his success in persuading General Figuereido to establish a Housies production line in Brazil.

When scene 4 opens four days have passed, but there are high hopes of being rescued; all help to pile up material on the snow that will identify them from the air. As they work, the talk is of the restaurants they know and of their favorite dishes. A plane is heard passing overhead—has it seen them? All dream of the first thing they will do when they get back, but gradually hope begins to fade. The talk turns to their present situation. Nan says she's seen Bob stealing and hiding food; others have seen him too. When he appears Bob seems slightly deranged: he complains of people whispering behind his back in the corridors of the fifty-ninth floor of the Housies building in Seattle. He swears to make big changes, threatening carnage: "et s'il faut qu'il y ait des cadavres . . ." (and if there have to be corpses . . .). On the other side of the stage Sue and Nan are preparing a stew from entrails and other bits of the corpses they had not so far dared to touch. As this comes to a boil, Bob collapses and dies; the end of this scene is marked by a starkly grotesque use of contrapuntal dialogue for ironic effect.

Six days later, with only six of them left, all hope of rescue has evaporated. Dick, confident in his mountaineering skills, is determined to find a way out on foot. There is some competition between Nan and Sue about who will accompany him. At the last minute it is Nan who goes; Sue and Jack are surprised to find their mutual affection returning. Meanwhile, both Ed and Bess are absorbed by past memories. A further nine days later scene 6 graphically demonstrates the bowel problems experienced by the four survivors (Dick and Nan have not returned). There is now much less talk of Housies and an absolute realism about their desperate situation. Jack declares his intention to abandon his career in business; Sue begins to glimpse the possibility of a new beginning with Jack. Bess, meanwhile, is incapable of facing the situation: her mind remains stuck in its old groove of tourism and shopping. They go to sleep prepared for a last attempt to escape in the morning. In the dark an avalanche covers them, killing Bess and Jack. The last scene takes place a week later. Ed and Sue are again preparing to leave. Ed gives her a terse account of how the Housies hierarchy was created. It is very different from that given by Bob and reveals Ed as a great survivor among ravening beasts (as he says, "il fallait manger" [I had to eat]). In order to keep up their spirits Ed and Sue discuss possible new beginnings if they succeed in reaching home. Ed confesses his fear of vertigo, and the last words are Sue telling Ed to step in her footprints as they leave.

Dramatic Technique in *L'Ordinaire*

L'Ordinaire is the first of a group of plays by Vinaver (whose composition happens to coincide with the decade of the 1980s) in which the plot or story element acquires a new importance. But it is combined with the systematic use of counterpoint, as developed in his earlier, more experimental plays, in order to achieve the effects of irony and allusive meaning. The experience of seeing this play should leave its audience sickened by the political injustice of the relationships that exist between the industrialized and the nonindustrialized countries, those who eat and those who are eaten. But nowhere does the play contain a scene of "protest": the effect is achieved entirely by irony and by implication. The method of counterpoint allows the playwright to exploit the dramatic medium in the way that is best suited to stage performance, that is, through enactment rather than discussion. To witness these overfed executives lovingly discussing the haute cuisine of a few privileged restaurants in a continent dominated by mass hunger carries a strong ironic charge; to see them doing so when they are unable to feed themselves because their umbilical cord to North America has been severed makes the revelation of their true situation even more flagrant.

The fundamental irony and motor of the play's dramatic force lie in the author's exploitation of the basic situation into which the executives are plunged when their plane comes down. With the sole exception of Sue, none of them wants to be in South America. Their only reason for being there is to make a quick profit and then retire to the comfort and security of Seattle. Their vision of the continent is limited to a succession of interviews with the military men in power. These interviews, the most recent of which is lovingly rehearsed at various points by Bob, are conducted like a game of poker. Their sole aim is to secure the best possible deal for Housies, and their strategy is to insist on talking only to the general (never to a subordinate) after canvassing information about his psychological peculiarities. Their policy, in other words, is to go straight to the top. Now they find themselves stuck at the top in quite a different sense, and the superficiality of their approach is revealed in its enormity. This outlook on the world is further revealed by their pathetic certainty that Reagan will come to their rescue and their recurrent terror of the guerrilla band supposedly out to take them hostage.

The play succeeds in evoking the group's survival on the mountainside, with vivid attention to concrete detail, while at the same time building up allusive references to everything beyond the mountainside. Vinaver exploits the allusive or poetic overtones that arise from intense concentration on simple bodily functions, such as eating and defecating, filling up and emptying out, so as to explore both the internal relationships of this little group and also their relationship with the world at large. The allusive method by which this is done relies on the use of dramatic contrasts. The most obvious of these is the ironic reversal of their situation: they move from a position of detachment from the problems of everyday survival on the continent (before the crash) to a position in which they experience in their own bodies the hunger and cold of those from whom they were hoping to make profits (afterward). Vinaver builds up different kinds of tension between the behavior of the characters and the reality of their situation. Some of the characters simply ignore the situation; Bob is particularly prone to this, and his inability to adjust to a situation in which he cannot order and be obeyed makes him an unsympathetic character to the audience. His vice presidents vary in the extent to which they continue to recognize his leadership, fight among themselves, or begin to act on their own initiatives. Vinaver here exploits the same behavior pattern as that developed by Shakespeare in his depiction of Alonso and his courtiers in *The Tempest*. In other cases characters struggle to adapt to the circumstances. By juxtaposing these different kinds of behavior and by crosscutting dialogues, Vinaver builds up his ironic or allusive commentary.

An example is the fourth scene, in which Bob collapses and dies. The last seven pages of this scene embody the death throes of Bob's empire: he has tried to cement a group of people entirely subordinate to his will, but ultimately they escape his control. The middle section of the scene presents, through its use of stage groupings, an image of this disintegration (*Théâtre II*, 339–42). Bob withdraws into the cabin, while Jack goes to work once again at the radio, Dick and Sue busy themselves with sewing knapsacks in another part of the stage, and a third group is made up by Ed and Nan, who are cutting up meat. Bess joins Jack and confides her worries about Bob: his wound has become infected, and his behavior seems strange to her. Jack reveals to Bess that Bob has been stealing food; she excuses him on the grounds of his deprived childhood and begs Jack to hush it up. In the two other groups the same revelation is being made (the three dialogues are intercut, all taking place simultaneously). When Nan informs Ed she is disappointed to find him retreating into male solidarity and insisting that they must keep quiet about it. As for Dick, always the most loyal of Bob's lieutenants, he simply refuses to believe it; he is too absorbed with preparing for his expedition—Bob has designated him as leader. The technique employed here is exactly the same as was used in the more experimental plays of the 1970s, such as *La Demande d'emploi:* it gives the audience a privileged view—they witness the simultaneous but separate development of the three conversations—and sets up resonances between different statements that are quite unintended by the characters but suggest additional meanings to the audience.

At this point Bob enters and is immediately aware that something is wrong. Instead of facing up to the present problems, he launches into a long tirade about whisperings in the corridors of his office building back home.

> For some time now I've been noticing people on the fifty-ninth floor
> slipping out from their offices into the corridors
> There's a rustling in the corridors a muffled murmuring
> Murmuring without cease
> Sarcasms and machinations

While this is going on of course none of the things that ought to be
done in the offices
Gets done

(Théâtre II, 342)[8]

This extraordinary displacement is rendered grotesquely comic by being
crosscut with dialogue between Nan and Sue as they begin to make a fire
out of Coca-Cola cases in order to stew some leftovers from the dead
bodies. The rest all gather around Bob; Jack is indifferent as Bob threatens
to make "corpses" of his staff, but both Ed and Dick take him seriously,
urge him to take a more considered approach. As they discuss the detailed
workings of the Housie Corporation's great global body, Nan comments,
fascinated on the different parts of the human body that are going into the
stew: liver, brains, kidney, even a testicle.

This contrapuntal effect reaches its most grotesque when Bob collapses, and the discussion around the cooking pot is crosscut with the
efforts by Bess, Jack, Dick, and Ed to revive him.

SUE: Just a minute or two more on the fire and it'll taste even better
ED: His heart's beating
NAN: Are you sure we can eat that?
SUE: I put in some brains as well
NAN: You're sure
JACK: His nostrils are moving
NAN: That it won't make us sick?
SUE: A ball look
NAN: Really
BESS: Praise the Lord
DICK: The wind's getting up
   Let's carry him into the cabin
SUE: Now we can call them
NAN: It's going to be difficult
SUE: No
NAN: To tell Mom
SUE: Nan Mister Lamb is breathing his last
NAN: This piece?
SUE: Taste
NAN: It's sweet and soft melts in the mouth
SUE: Liver

ED: His pulse is beating
NAN: Hmm
  And this all wrapped up in fat
BESS: Bob
DICK: His lips
JACK: Are moving
SUE: A kidney

(Théâtre II, 345–46)[9]

This scene effectively forestalls any temptation the audience might have to see Bob's death in a tragic light; in performance it can hardly avoid provoking laughter, albeit of a grim variety. By juxtaposing those parts of the body that give signs of life (lips, nostrils, etc.) with those that taste good (kidneys, liver, etc.), the sequences place the death of this one individual in the context of a cyclical view of life, with the death of the old nourishing the growth of the new. The sequence naturally sparks off allusions, for the audience, to the generation gap (a regular theme emerging from encounters between Nan and Bob at earlier points in the play). Nan has had a difficult relationship with her own father, always feeling that he was "devouring" her (325); now her pleasure in the taste of the meat exacts a kind of revenge (although the fear of parental authority is still strong—she wonders how she will be able to tell her mother). The excitement she finds in the process of cooking and eating also recalls ironically the discussion of haute cuisine and boasting about favorite restaurants of Bob, Bess, and the others at the start of the same scene. In addition, the audience cannot help recalling Bob's threat to create corpses and reflecting that he who prided himself on devouring others is next in line for the cooking pot.

The depiction of the situation in *L'Ordinaire* builds on the experimental method of Vinaver's plays of the previous decade. In *Les Travaux et les jours,* for example, the fictional setting of the office was perfectly respected, but the intercutting of the characters' dialogue introduced elements from their private as well as their public lives in ways that would not have been possible for a playwright concerned with maintaining the naturalist illusion and to show only what might happen in any normal office. In *L'Ordinaire* Vinaver is again strictly selective. He places great emphasis on the details of ordinary, everyday life: for most of scene 6 the four remaining characters are crouching in the snow with their pants down, coping with the problem of loose bowels, which has followed the chronic constipation of the first weeks. But many of the essential activities necessary for survival on the mountainside are omitted. Where something is depicted in detail, as in the case of the stew being cooked at the end of scene 4, it is done in order to achieve a particular dramatic effect, not in order to generate an illusion of reality. Naturalism is in any case excluded, since the act of eating human flesh is not subject to the same kind of authentic presentation on stage that is possible for the act of drinking tea or eating conventional food. Rather than trying to persuade an audience that they are really eating the remains of their associates, the actors have the task (perhaps a more difficult one) of conveying the paradoxical duality of the act: both its enormity and its ordinariness.

In aiming for this result Vinaver was very clear that the function of his play was not to put the capitalist system on trial so as to weigh the pros and cons and pass judgment on it. He describes the process, rather, as one of *"le montage et le démontage."* The play's seven scenes are termed *morceaux* (which could be translated as "bits" or "pieces") by the author, whose gloss on this term is as follows: *"Les morceaux* is the state of a body after an accident; it describes what does not automatically hold together—something that must be built, stuck, put together" (*Mémoire sur mes travaux,* 24, 44).[10] The structure of the play thus mirrors the pattern of events presented in it: the characters of the play will try to reassemble the remains of broken objects, bodies, lives, in a way that makes sense to them. They will succeed to a limited degree, but these attempts will often suggest quite different meanings for the audience.

This is what Vinaver meant when he talked of *montage* and *démontage:*

> The process of *montage* involves revealing, on the surface of the text, all the familiar elements that make up the [capitalist] system, whether orderly or disorderly, in such a way that their potential for terror and pity and strangeness bursts forth. The process of *démontage* involves the work done by the text as it reveals intimate life in its minutest pulsations interacting with the large-scale results of the socioeconomic machine. (*Mémoire sur mes travaux,* 24)[11]

In other words the structure of the play needed to show how the most intimate details of human behavior can serve the interests of "the system" or be conditioned by it. This was important if reality was to be respected, since a simple denunciation of the system achieves nothing more than a sense of self-satisfaction and superiority on the part of both playwright and audience. "What these plays reveal, by means of *montage* and *démontage*, is how the system functions, how it is constantly degenerating and regenerating, throwing its agents 'overboard' or leaving them to go 'into reverse' or devouring them as part of its 'everyday fare.'"[12] The result aimed for is a comic vision: "This comic vision of the way the system functions has the peculiarity of being produced by one of the system's devoted agents; a bit as if Harlequin, without abandoning his character, had taken on, for one of his escapades, the status of author" (*Mémoire sur mes travaux*, 24).[13] This emphasis on the comic vision recalls his view of the writer's role as jester (see *Ecrits sur le théâtre*, 316) and implies a performance style that is not to be reconciled with naturalism.

The reviews of the first production of the play suggest that the actors did not entirely succeed in finding an appropriately large or presentational style of performance. Anne Ubersfeld felt that only Anouk Grinberg (Vinaver's youngest daughter) came close to it (*Vinaver dramaturge*, 63). This is significant, since it was the only production of one of his plays in which Vinaver himself took a hand. When rehearsals began, in January 1983, he was halfway through teaching his first university seminar in dramatic analysis. For this seminar he had developed an original method of close textual reading, which he wanted to try out on a play of his own. The method involved adding dynamics to the text, rather as they might be added to a musical score (see pp. 104–5), and he felt that these could provide a rigorous guide to the actors, helping them to understand the rhythms of his text. A sequence of photographs reproduced in *L'Annuel du théâtre, 1982–1983* (181–91) shows the cast during the initial read-throughs (known in French as *travail à table*). This phase of the work lasted for a couple of weeks, and it was here that Vinaver made his directorial contribution.

The visual aspects of the production were the responsibility of Alain Françon and of the designer Gérard Schlosser, who chose to reproduce the setting of the action in naturalistic detail. An intensely realistic wrecked fuselage was constructed, surrounded by an equally realistic snowfield, set on a steep rake. The actors experienced great difficulty in bringing together the rhythmic, almost poetic approach to the text that they had worked on during the *travail à table* and the naturalistic behavior forced on them by the stage set. The result was a lack of conviction in performance, although most of the reviewers were favorable, and many commented that the strength of the text was clear despite the weaknesses of the production. This experience convinced Vinaver of two things: that he did not want to direct his own work and that a stage set attempting to give the illusion of reality was fundamentally harmful to a sensitive realization of his text.

The latter is a problem faced by actors and directors of all of Vinaver's plays; the necessity of finding an appropriate nonnaturalistic acting style is forced on the performer by the extensive use of counterpoint in the dialogue. Part of what is said remains strictly within the limits of what might really be said by people in a given situation. But in *L'Ordinaire* the playwright is not content with a simple evocation of human behavior after a disaster: he is constantly displacing the center of interest onto something else. This something else is the shifting focus of the characters' minds, as they attempt to come to terms with their new situation. To a greater or lesser extent, the words of each character include passages that no one would voice out loud, though they might think them. This gives to the play a characteristic note reminiscent of Woolf or Joyce. In the last article he published before his death Adamov wrote that he dreamed of a theater in which every statement and action was almost what would be expected in real life, but not quite: a slight discrepancy would be constantly perceptible, a minimal distance from reality creating enough of a gap for the audience to be nudged beyond the familiar preoccupation with realism into reflection on the implications of what was being presented ("Presque—le théâtre et le rêve"). Vinaver's dialogue achieves exactly this effect.

In summing up how this is done it is useful to return to Vinaver's account of the function of myth in his work and to his phrase "the mythic shuttle," coined to convey the idea of a movement backward and forward: "a come-and-go between contemporary reality (that amorphous territory, fragmented and devoid of landmarks) and the ordered world as it is recounted in myth" (*Mémoire sur mes travaux,* 33).[14] Every character in *L'Ordinaire* experiences the need to make this movement from the immediate to the mythical and back, because their experience of ordinary reality on the snowfield is, quite literally, "amorphous, fragmented, and devoid of landmarks." Because their normal world has broken up, and they cannot be sure where they are, they have recourse to external structures of explanation, all more or less mythical. Bob mythologizes his meetings with generals and persuades himself that he, as a captain of industry, has

U N

(L'intérieur de la cabine de l'avion. Bess, Bob, Dick et Joe,
autour d'une table, jouent aux cartes. Pat, à une autre table,
tape à la machine. Sur une couchette, Ed dort. Sur une autre
couchette, Sue, allongée, lit un magazine, la tête sur les ge-
noux de Jack, assis dans l'angle. Nan se fait les ongles des
pieds. Jim, par intermittence, va et vient entre la cabine et
le poste de pilotage.)

(1) L'ÉTAT DES CHOSES

Sue   C'est fini Jack *LP*
C'est la fin de notre histoire

Jack   Mais *LP* Santiago est une ville sinistre

Sue   J'aimerais que tu ne reviennes pas encore une fois là-dessus
Dans le fond/toi aussi /
Tu sais que c'est fini

Jack   Tu ne m'aimes plus ?

Sue   Non
Toi non plus *LP*
On a conclu tout ça avant de partir
C'était bien
Maintenant tu essaies de tout réouvrir

Jack   Santiago est une ville où il n'y a rien *LP*
Je ne peux pas t'abandonner à Santiago *LP*
Je te ramène à Seattle de Seattle tu iras où tu voudras je
te paierai le voyage pour où tu voudras en attendant
tu réfléchiras   ] d'un trait

2

Sue   Tu ne m'abandonnes pas
          C'est moi qui me taille mais pour que tu te mettes ça dans la tête

Jack   Il n'y a rien absolument rien à Santiago tu aurais dû rester à Rio
          J'oublie que tu n'as pas aimé Rio
          Tu es la première personne que je connaisse qui n'ait pas été
                 happée par le charme de Rio

Sue   Je ne cherche pas les beautés touristiques

Jack   Tu aurais pu rester à Buenos Aires
          A Buenos Aires il se passe des choses

Sue   Je veux un endroit quelconque Jack où tu ne seras pas

Notations

LP   *légère pause*

/   *détacher*

∫   *enchaîner*

∧   *accent, intensité*

•   *rime, assonance*

—   *analogie*

The first two pages of Michel Vinaver's 1983 play *L'Ordinaire,* with Vinaver's notations indicating slight pause *(légère pause)*; break *(détacher)*; link or run in *(enchaîner)*; emphasis *(accent, intensité)*; rhyme or assonance *(rime, assonance)*; and similar inflection *(analogie)*.

a special place in the affections of Ronald Reagan. Faced with the prospect of the destruction of his company's executive committee, he feverishly reaffirms his faith in its worldwide survival. Bess mythologizes the cannibal act by reference to the Christian sacrament of the Body of Christ. Pat mythologizes the former attractions of her now useless legs, and Nan mythologizes the power of older men.

Unlike some of the other plays, this one is not structured on a preexisting myth (though there are obvious allusions to the myth of the Waste Land). References to preexisting myths are minimal. But the whole play is permeated with the problems to which myth is commonly supposed to provide answers: the harking back to origins, the need to explain the workings of fate, the significance to be attached to human life, especially in the rituals surrounding the absorption of nourishment and the disposal of the dead. When discussing the relationship between myth and theater at the outset of his play-writing career Vinaver had explained that he saw theater in terms of an initiation, or rite of passage (see pages 6–7). He had recourse to the same language in describing *L'Ordinaire:* "In *L'Ordinaire* the rite of passage is via anthropophagy.... The action of the play consists in the progressive drive toward a new way of being. It is an initiation journey, here again, alternating with the opposite drive (rather die than change...)" (*Mémoire sur mes travaux,* 32–33).[15]

For each character on the mountainside there is the challenge of what the author terms "an initiation journey" *(un parcours initiatique),* and to come through this initiation successfully necessitates a reexamination of a whole worldview, including beliefs about origins and purpose. The audience's attention is drawn to this by several passages in which myths or stories are explicitly discussed. In the final scene of the play, for example, when Sue and Ed are about to make a last bid for freedom and a new beginning, what they discuss is the origin of Housies. Ed sums it up in a terse half-page as a power struggle between three men, each trying to devour the other two: Bob proved to have the largest appetite and the sharpest teeth. Sue contrasts this story with the myth of origins she had heard, years before, from an old Mayan chief in Mexico. He had told her how the world had been born from "the arse-hole of a mouse," and Sue had been sure he was making fun of her. But after her forty-two-day initiation in the Andes she begins to wonder if it was not entirely appropriate as a means of expressing American civilization:

SUE: Through the arse-hole of a mouse
The birth of Mickey Housies
Its history and its end.

(*Théâtre II*, 370)[16]

NOTES

1. Nous sommes passés d'Homère à Hésiode; nostalgie, fêlure.
2. Dans *Par-dessus bord*, les personnages avaient une identité du début à la fin. Dans *A La Renverse*, ils n'ont pas de contours. La tentative consiste à montrer de nombreux personnages (par six acteurs) s'évanouissant.
3. La pièce envisage le capitalisme comme moteur à renversement. Chaque catastrophe le fait avancer.
4. L'acte de bronzer consiste à se laisser pénétrer . . . la pénétration solaire en tant que diffuse apporte un plaisir mois paroxystique mais aussi gratifiant d'autant qu'il ne comporte aucun facteur culpabilisant.
5. A noter que tout plaisir est d'autant plus intense qu'y entre de façon complémentaire la composante qui lui est opposée à savoir la peur.
6. Le couple Bénédicte-Pellepain: deux "héroines," chacune occupant l'un des deux hémisphères de la rêverie populaire—figures féminines—la princesse (tragique) et la bergère (épique).
7. Mister Lamb je suis sûre que Papa serait d'accord s'il savait qu'il ne reste que quelques olives et quelques crackers
Il serait d'accord avec ce qu'a dit Pat
8. Ça fait quelque temps que j'observe un glissement de la population du cinquante-neuvième étage des bureaux vers les couloirs
Les couloirs bruissent c'est un murmure feutré
Un murmure ininterrompu
De sarcasmes et de machinations
Pendant ce temps bien sûr rien de ce qui doit se faire dans les bureaux
Ne se fait
9.   SUE: Encore une minute sur le feu ça sera encore plus savoureux
ED: Le coeur bat
NAN: Tu es sûre qu'on peut manger ça?
SUE: J'y ai mis aussi une cervelle
NAN: Tu es sûre
JACK: Les narines remuent
NAN: Que ca ne va pas nous rendre malades?
SUE: Une couille regarde
NAN: Vraiment
BESS: Dieu soit loué
DICK: Le vent s'est levé
Transportons-le dans la cabine

SUE: Maintenant on peut les appeler
NAN: Ce sera difficile
SUE: Mais non
NAN: De raconter à Maman
SUE: Nan Mister Lamb vit ses derniers moments
NAN: Ce morceau?
SUE: Goûte
NAN: C'est doux c'est fondant les dents s'amusent dedans
SUE: Le foie
ED: Le pouls bat
NAN: Hmm
    Et avec cette grosse enveloppe de graisse tout autour
BESS: Bob
DICK: Ses lèvres
JACK: Remuent
SUE: Un rein

10. Les morceaux, c'est l'état d'un corps après accident; c'est ce qui ne tient pas ensemble d'emblée; c'est ce qui s'assemble, se colle, se monte.

11. Le montage, c'est faire apparaître, sur une surface qui est celle du texte, tous les éléments familiers qui le composent dans un ordre, ou un désordre, tel que leur charge de terreur et de pitié et d'étrangeté éclate. Le démontage c'est, par le travail que fait le texte, mettre en évidence l'intime, dans ses pulsations les plus ténues, en interaction avec les effets lourds de la machine socio-économique.

12. Ce que les pièces dévoilent, par voie de montage et de démontage, c'est comment le Système fonctionne, comment il ne cesse de se dégrader et de se régénérer, en jetant ses agents "par-dessus bord" ou en les laissant tomber "à la renverse," en les consommant pour en faire son "ordinaire."

13. La vision comique sur le fonctionnement du Système a ceci de particulier qu'elle provient d'un agent dévoué du Système; on peut penser à Arlequin qui, sans abandonner son statut de personnage agissant, adopterait, le temps d'une escapade, le statut d'auteur.

14. Un va-et-vient entre l'actualité (ce territoire indistinct, morcelé, sans repères) et l'ordre du monde tel qu'il est dit dans les mythes.

15. Dans *L'Ordinaire,* le rite de passage emprunte la voie de l'anthropophagie. . . . L'action de la pièce réside dans la poussée progressive vers une nouvelle façon d'être. Parcours initiatique, ici encore, contrarié par une poussée inverse (plutôt la mort que le changement . . .).

16. SUE: Par le trou du cul d'une souris
La naissance de Mickey Housies
Son histoire et sa fin

Chapter 6

Neighbors, Justice, and Television

Les Voisins

In his commentary on his own work Vinaver classes *Les Voisins* with the chamber theater plays. The reason he gives for this classification has to do with their intimate focus and the size of the cast in each play: as he points out, there is a clear difference between the chamber plays (maximum cast of five) and what he calls the "symphonic plays," most of which have casts in the twenties or thirties and whose minimum is the eleven of *L'Ordinaire* (see *Mémoire sur mes travaux*, 42). There are other, more telling points of similarity between *Les Voisins* and the chamber plays of the 1970s, especially the focus on intimate life. *Les Voisins* centers on the same kind of small "family" group as the earlier chamber plays and, like them, relies on a subtle, microscopic examination of the psychological mechanisms at work in close human relationships. In this kind of group the characters establish their identity by contrast with one another more than through their relationships with the outside world (though these are always evoked). The dynamics of the group are generated by the shifting relationships of the individuals within it, ranging from love, loyalty, and trust to vulnerability, treachery, and hatred.

The four characters of *Les Voisins* live side by side in two semidetached houses with a shared terrace: on one side Laheu and his son Ulysse, on the other Blason and his daughter Alice. The two fathers both have respectable office jobs: Laheu works for the Universal Biscuit Company, and Blason works for an insurance company. Their children are in their early twenties and dream of setting up a restaurant together. Blason's wife was killed in a car accident when Alice was still a baby; Laheu's wife left him several years before. The result is that the four of them have come to rely on one another. On special occasions they eat together on the communal terrace and share their most treasured secrets, notably the fact that Blason is gradually building up a small stock of gold bars, which he hides under one of the paving stones of the terrace. Alice and Ulysse have always been best friends and plan to get married when they have set up in business.

The events of the play are divided into three acts. In the first an amicable shared dinner takes place on the terrace. Elisa, Ulysse's dog that has been part of the families' life for sixteen years (since her birth on this very terrace), has just died of old age. Alice and Ulysse have buried her in a favorite woodland spot, and the two fathers and their children gather for a funeral supper. At the end of the evening Blason shows Laheu his latest gold bar, his fifth, and the two men stow it with the others under the terrace, discussing plans for their children's future. Act 2 covers a period of twelve months in ten short sequences. It begins on the day after Blason's house has been torn apart by thieves, who have stolen the gold, and it shows the gradual estrangement of the two fathers, as each comes to suspect the other of trying to ruin him. It gradually emerges that the theft was the work of a local gang working for a certain Daphné with whom Ulysse had done business; suspicion falls heavily upon Ulysse, though he denies it. At the end of the act Blason and Laheu appear to have fallen out irrevocably, even coming to blows. The third act takes place a few weeks later; the two fathers have unexpectedly made it up and gone into the antiques business together. They now live in adjoining huts and sell their antiques at the flea market. The children are still with them and have set up a stand selling frankfurters and chips. They have acquired a new puppy. Blason travels the country buying up old furniture, which Laheu restores. In an old dresser brought back by Blason Laheu discovers a cache of gold coins; they decide to give it back to the woman who had sold them the dresser. As the play ends, Ulysse is brought in by Alice having made a suicide attempt.

As in the earlier chamber plays, Vinaver has adopted a story that is deliberately anecdotal, banal, apparently shapeless. It is the opposite of a "well-made play"—there are unexplained mysteries and ends that do not tie up, and the play's peripeteia do not have the careful preparation that one expects in a well-crafted domestic play. But its anecdotal surface is deceptive, hiding a great thematic richness and a comic demythologizing of what "goes without saying." This is one of Vinaver's most frankly comic plays, suggesting a parallel with Chekhov that the reviewers did not fail to pick up. It is also one of the few plays by Vinaver to have received universal critical approval. Its production by Alain Françon at Théâtre Ouvert's small theater in Paris coincided with the publication of his complete plays in two volumes. For the production and the publication he won the Ibsen prize, awarded annually for outstanding achievement in the French theater.

The qualities that were praised in the play were its humor, its encyclopedic ability to reflect the texture of ordinary French life, and its psychological complexity. Jean-Loup Rivière, who wrote a preface to the complete plays, suggested that the textual richness of Vinaver's work made him the cousin of Jacques Tati:

> Vinaver's theater constitutes a sort of catalog of Frenchness. Events, objects and expressions are picked out and woven into the texture of his plays so as to form a sort of museum of contemporary French ethnography. Executive unemployment; Czech cinema; hypermarkets; the pill; happenings; the Loterie Nationale; pollution; . . . a whole series of objects whose purpose is not to provide a background: they are the very substance of his plays. In their manner of presentation these objects become slightly strange. A space remains around them, they are not dissolved and re-formed, they retain their freshness and the smell of their roots. The comic quality of Vinaver's plays certainly stems from this way of seizing on objects or facts and lends him a certain family resemblance to Tati. If the characters in Tati's films started to speak, they would speak like those of Vina (let's call him that, just for the space of a paragraph). (*Théâtre I*, 17)[1]

Behind the figures of Blason and Laheu lurk the ghosts of Flaubert's Bouvard and Pécuchet, and in this play, more than any of the others, one detects the author's admiration for the *Dictionnaire des idées reçues,* Flaubert's great catalog of the banalities of nineteenth-century French everyday life.

But for all its similarities with the chamber plays *Les Voisins* also displays significant differences, and consideration of these will help to clarify its place in Vinaver's work as a whole. The most significant difference is the introduction of a "whodunit" element, something that is to be found in all of his later plays. In other words, he introduces a story line that requires the notion of a progression in time and renders impossible the exclusive emphasis on the present moment, which was a feature of, for example, *La Demande d'emploi.* But in doing so he does not abandon the principle of multiple viewpoint, nor does he allow the story to unfold in a simple unilinear manner. The second act of *Les Voisins* shows the audience brief, almost random glimpses of the events of the year following the theft. Within each episode we understand perfectly why the characters behave the way they do, but the events of separate episodes often seem to contradict one another. Vinaver is using a very Brechtian technique in this act, constantly surprising his audience, asking them to reconsider what had been clear in the previous scene. In the fourth scene, for example, Blason attempts to convince Laheu that Ulysse could not possibly be guilty of the theft; in the following scene he argues the opposite case.

The other major difference is in his treatment of the characters in *Les Voisins*. The characters of the earlier chamber plays all possess a representative quality. This is not to say that they are unconvincing—but when considering Fage in *La Demande d'emploi* an audience perceives not only the individual case but also the general problem of the unemployed executive. In Philippe of *Dissident, il va sans dire* they see the general problems afflicting young people in France; in the characters of *Les Travaux et les jours* they see the conditions that typically affect the lives of office workers. For *Les Voisins* Vinaver has chosen to create characters that do not have the same representative quality, being very much more idiosyncratic, more extreme, and hence more comic. Significantly, they are not portrayed in their place of work until the very end of the play, and this helps to emphasize their individual characteristics rather than those factors that make them representative of white-collar workers.

The development in Vinaver's writing can be attributed partly to his reflections on two adaptations he worked on in the early 1980s: *The Suicide* by Erdman and *Summerfolk* by Gorky. In an interview commenting on what attracted him about Erdman's play he commented on "that thing that Erdman can do and I cannot, and which I am striving for: the use of extreme exaggeration" (*Théâtre I*, 32).[2] Erdman's comedy certainly makes a freer use of the grotesque than is common in Vinaver's work. He is able to set up a situation that would seem to demand a highly melodramatic outcome and then divert it into an unexpected channel for humorous or satirical effect. Simon Podsekalnikov, the character who decides to commit suicide, finds that everyone wants to make use of his gesture; suddenly he is transformed, losing his sense of despair and isolation now that everyone wants him. The inconsequential (and somewhat unbelievable) story of Erdman's play is made to secrete a truth about social relationships that is nonetheless telling for arising out of a grotesque situation. Moreover, there is nothing in *The Suicide* that is fabulous or out of the ordinary: the events of the play all respect the humdrum reality of *le quotidien*. By his own admission, then, Vinaver saw in Erdman's use of *grossissement du trait* (exaggeration of a trait) a technique that he felt he needed to appropriate. *L'Ordinaire,* written the year after he had adapted *The Suicide,* had shown that he *was* capable of this; in *Les Voisins* he extended what he had learned into the field of comedy. The theme of the hoard of gold, for example, is presented quite naively (and rather surprisingly given the setting of a suburban villa) by having Blason hide his gold under the terrace then lose it then find gold again in unusual (though perfectly ordinary) circumstances. He is similarly able to present greater extremes of behavior in the relationship between Blason and Laheu than had been the case in the chamber plays of the 1970s.

His work on *Summerfolk* by Gorky (performed at the Comédie Française in 1983, directed by Jacques Lassalle) also helped to enhance and confirm methods of dramatic composition that he had developed on his own initiative. Of Gorky's play he wrote: "The play is full of discussions, and the ideas they debate are no longer topical for us. But Gorky's treatment of these discussions and of the situations and actions that accompany them, a contrapuntal treatment founded on the principle of the theme and variation, and of the intercutting of these themes and their variations, gives birth to material whose richness and associative power are limitless" (*Théâtre I,* 32–33).[3] None of the characters in Gorky's play is remarkable as an individual, but from the play as a whole there emerges that "group voice" identified by Raymond Williams as the great strength of Chekhovian naturalism and through which it is possible for the playwright to orchestrate the contrapuntal resonances evoked by Vinaver in this comment. Moreover, since the ideas and themes introduced into *Les Voisins* are so firmly rooted in the realities of French life today, the play can legitimately expect its subject matter, as well as its treatment, to be of interest to a contemporary French audience.

The themes that interweave to form the fabric of this play are of two different kinds. First, there are the themes drawn from ordinary, everyday experience of the world, the same themes that recur in most of Vinaver's plays: themes associated with the most fundamental realities of life like eating, cooking, buying, selling (or exchanging), being born, dying, finding work, the conditions of work, unemployment, etc. As is common with Vinaver, they often emerge in just this form of contrasted pairs of opposites but are always expressed through the concrete, lived experience of the characters on stage. The second kind of thematic material is more abstract and begins with the title of the play: neighbors. The notion of "neighborliness" is explored through a complex set of variations on the theme of the double. At the start of the play the two households of Laheu and Blason appear like a mirror image of one another: it is what they have in common that is emphasized. They are both single-parent families, they share the same life-style, the same social status, the same terrace, the same memories, the same sadness at the death of the same dog who has been their shared pet for sixteen years. But, as the play progresses, the theme of the double emerges in other forms. First, the audience begins to distinguish the differences between the two households, coming to see them as complementary rather than as mirror images. In their attitudes toward money, for example, Blason is a hoarder, and Laheu a spendthrift; Blason has economic power, whereas Laheu does not. But this appreciation of the pair of men is reversed after the theft, when all Blason's savings are gone and Laheu is able to offer him hospitality, shelter, and help with reconstruction. There is a similar reversal in the way they relate to one another's children. At first Blason is loud in the praises of Laheu's son, and Laheu is appreciative of Blason's daughter. But, as the police inquest casts increasingly heavy suspicion on Ulysse, these attitudes tip over into their opposites.

The theme of the double is not limited to the characters but reappears at every level of the plot. In the unfolding of the story the theme is used to suggest a cyclical progression: the play opens with the death of the family pet and the evocation of the day of her birth by Alice and Ulysse, who had witnessed it together as children; by the third act they have a new puppy. The gold that is hoarded in the first act and stolen in the second reappears in the form of the discovery in the old dresser in the third act. The same cyclical dualism emerges from the fragments of information we gather about the economic and political events of the municipality in which they live, which is dominated by the struggle for power between two rich businessmen, Delorge and Jonc. Blason has links with Jonc and Laheu with Delorge, so that each is able to use his influence to harm the other. At a more general level Vinaver's play explores the nature of the neighborly relationship, suggesting that it has a particularly intense quality: it is not like a marriage, in which (theoretically, at least) the interests of the two partners are dissolved into one. It implies that the two parties retain complete autonomy. Yet at the same time it can be a relationship in which two people come to rely utterly upon one another: it is on this note of complementarity that the play ends, with Laheu and Blason pooling their different skills in order to set up a business together.

But, despite the undoubted thematic richness of the play, an analysis restricted to themes risks obscuring the novelty of the play in relation to all of Vinaver's previous works, especially its comic qualities. The comedy was mentioned by almost every reviewer, for example: "From this comic tale, which might have been inspired by Labiche, Vinaver has constructed a strange contemporary vaudeville—acid, disturbing, very subtle, and wildly funny" (Jacques Nerson, *Figaro Magazine,* 15 November 1986).[4] The kind of comedy most characteristically associated with Vinaver's work is the comedy of irony—comedy of a rather intellectual kind, which raises a smile rather than a laugh. But the performances of *Les Voisins* raised laughs. This was because Vinaver had followed the lesson learned from Erdman and made both his characters and his events more unpredictable, the reversals more unexpected, and the reactions more grotesque. In the course of doing so, some of the sense of absolute faithfulness to everyday life was lost; at certain points in the play events seem outrageous or unlikely—in a word, theatrical. The discovery of the second hoard of gold, for example, seems "too good to be true" until one realizes that it is being used to make a comment about particular ways of telling stories and of shaping experience.

Reading the reviews of the first production, one detects a note of surprise: Vinaver was known as the leading French dramatist, a serious writer whom the critics did not associate with comedy, and yet they had clearly found the performance a joyous experience. Some of the credit must go to Alain Françon, whose production for Théâtre Ouvert established a speed and lightness of touch uncommon in professional realizations of Vinaver's plays. The cast (Raymond Jourdan as Blason, Robert Rimbaud as Laheu, Anouk Grinberg as Alice, and Charles Berling as Ulysse) were uniformly strong and managed to convey both comedy and emotional power (a combination French actors often find difficult). The set by Yannis Kokkos was a masterpiece of simplicity, and the scene changes were as near instantaneous as possible. The production was cosponsored by the Théâtre Eclaté of Annecy, the Comédie de Caen, and the Grenier de Toulouse and toured to these theaters after its run in Paris.

In this play, for the first time, Vinaver allowed himself to treat reality in a playful way. What appears to be a simple enough story is constantly being questioned, turned back on itself, forced to change direction. The abstract pattern of the double is constantly clamoring for the audience's attention, and the narrative structure itself is repeatedly problematized. The detective story interest that is aroused in act 2 by the inquest into the theft, for example, is left unsatisfied because the story refuses to conform to the pattern of the *policier* (detective thriller). Most telling of all, the relationship between the private world of the neighbors and the larger social reality is not established with the same thoroughness as in Vinaver's other plays. The machinations of Delorge and Jonc (and the bearing they have on the relationship between Blason and Laheu) remain shrouded in mystery, alluded to only in such a fragmentary way that it is difficult for the audience to establish any meaningful links between the two worlds. The dialectical movement established, for example, in *L'Ordinaire*—between the small world of the Housies executives and the larger economic realities outside—has no equivalent in *Les Voisins*.

The result is that, while the play gains in comic unpredictability, it loses something of the socially representative quality admired by Rivière. This is significant since it was clearly not the author's intention in writing this play to weaken the social aspect of his dramaturgical method. In the passage in which he justifies its inclusion among his chamber plays he argues:

> In fact, while it is true that each of these five plays concentrates on the internal events that stir up a small family or professional cell, it is also true to say that their fundamental aim is not so different from that of the symphonic plays: to reveal the porosity between this intimate nucleus of life and the larger pulsations of the world to which this nucleus belongs. *(Mémoire sur mes travaux, 42)*[5]

But, rather than emphasizing this "porosity," *Les Voisins* in fact shows something slightly different: a small, rather unusually constituted group reacting in a variety of ways, some predictable, some surprising, to the pressures exerted upon it by events that are beyond the control or even the comprehension of its members. This makes for comedy of an unusual kind in Vinaver's work since the focus is almost exclusively on what he calls the "internal events." External events ("the larger pulsations of the world") are evoked in passing, but the play does not offer an insight into the workings of French society at large in the same way as was achieved, for example, by *Les Travaux et les jours*.

Justice and l'objecteur

In the course of the 1980s a new theme emerged in Vinaver's work: the theme of justice. Both *Portrait d'une femme* and *L'Emission de télévision* are centrally concerned with the processes of justice in French society. But the introduction of this new thematic material also marks a return to the preoccupations of the postwar years, when Vinaver was setting out on his writing career. *Portrait d'une femme* is set in 1953 (the only play by Vinaver not set in present time), and the theme of justice is accompanied by a complementary theme, that of *l'objecteur*, which had been central to Vinaver's novel of that title, published in 1951. In these two plays can be seen a résumé of the major themes and techniques of the playwright's work over four decades.

Portrait d'une femme was written at the same time as *Les Voisins*, and the circumstances of its writing provide an interesting insight into the processes of the playwright's mind. While turning out his attic, he discovered a file in which he had collected a set of newspaper cuttings relating to the trial of Pauline Dubuisson, convicted after a famous trial in 1953 of having murdered her lover and condemned to hard labor for life. The rediscovery of these press reports reawakened Vinaver's interest in the case and in the figure of Pauline Dubuisson. He did not attempt to trace her or try to make her the subject of biographical research; he had no desire to solve the mystery of her motives for the crime nor to use it as the pretext for a detective story. What struck him forcibly on rereading the reports of the case (which included large extracts of the speeches for the prosecution, defense, etc.) was the mutual incomprehension between the court and the accused. Neither had any understanding of the other: each could be seen to be functioning according to a set of precise and complex mechanisms—psychological, legal, ideological—but neither was able to engage at any point with the other.

Vinaver saw powerful dramatic potential in this flagrant failure to connect. As a kind of discipline, ensuring respect for the realities of the historical event, he decided that he would include in his play every one of the speeches reported to have taken place in court in the set of cuttings that he had kept from *Le Monde* of 1953. The effect of this is to include certain elements that remain opaque and to create a slight sense of strangeness in the language, since the historical distance is noticeable in certain turns of phrase used by the judge and lawyers. Intercalated with the court proceedings, Vinaver wrote a series of fictional "flashback" scenes in which the audience sees the life of his murderer, whom he named Sophie Auzanneau, in the years leading up to her crime. The language spoken in these scenes is the everyday language of young people, with no particular effort made to reconstruct a 1940s style, and so the impression of failure to intersect between court and accused is heightened.

In the way he has chosen to write this play Vinaver has created an unusual form of dramatic "present time." The events and encounters shown on stage range over a period of more than six years, but all take place within the context of the trial at the Paris court of Assizes, so that they appear as flashbacks. A similar technique has often been used in the theater, but is usually employed to amplify the *account* of an event by recreating it "as it happened." This method was used, for example, by Roger Planchon for his first play, *La Remise* (1962). Vinaver's method in *Portrait d'une femme* is more like that he used in *La Demande d'emploi,* switching abruptly from one scene to another, often running several scenes simultaneously, so that it can be quite difficult working out which statements belong in which scene, especially when Sophie is participating in more than one at the same time. The method allows for a given statement or action to contradict or temper another and for resonances of meaning connecting ostensibly disparate things. In order to be sure that this simultaneity is preserved in production Vinaver has written an unusually prescriptive set of stage directions: he specifies that there be no fixed scenery but that the scenic elements be brought on and off or moved around by a stagehand in full view of the audience while the action continues (the play must be performed without interval). The scenic elements belong to what the author calls two sharply contrasted registers: one consists of colorless everyday objects such as tables and chairs, which are purely functional; the other is the "hyperrealistic" copy of bits of the Paris court of Assizes spread around so as to form a sort of incomplete jigsaw puzzle.

The play's field of dramatic action is predominantly linguistic: it is built up through a struggle between different idioms, each carrying its own implicit value judgments and ideological presuppositions. Broadly, they fall into two registers (corresponding to the two "registers" of scenic elements): on the one hand, the rather formal language of the members of the judiciary and, on the other, the informal speech of the family and friends of Sophie Auzanneau. We will consider first the judiciary. There are four of them: the Presiding Judge at the Paris court of Assizes; the Public Prosecutor (Avocat Général); Maître Lubet, the Avocat de la Partie Civile, who is the lawyer acting on behalf of the murdered man and his family; and Maître Cancé, the Avocat de la Défense, the lawyer acting on behalf of Sophie. In addition to this there is a brief intervention by a psychiatric doctor. The language employed by these characters is designed to display an ostensible concern for establishing the precise facts of the case. The opening of the play shows the Presiding Judge rehearsing Sophie's exact movements on the night of the murder: how she climbed the stairs to Xavier's flat, rang the bell, entered, had a brief exchange of words with him, then took from the pocket of her raincoat a revolver with which she shot him three times. The rhetoric of the court is governed by the need to represent its workings as objective, impartial, concerned only with hard facts. Maître Lubet states this explicitly.

> Petty of me perhaps but I'm concerned with the facts
> I stick to the facts
>
> *(New French Plays, 8)*[6]

But the processes of the law demand that these facts be not treated with the scientific objectivity that is claimed. Rather, they are placed in a perspective that can only be tendentious, since the aim of the legal process is to arrive at a point where responsibility can be assigned—in other words, where something much more than the mere facts will emerge. For the law to pass sentence a motive must be found, and in a case being tried for murder the motive is crucial, since the judgment must depend on whether or not the shooting was carried out with premeditation. Immediately following the Presiding Judge's rehearsal of Xavier's death, the Public Prosecutor repeats the facts in the following terms.

> Yes he collapses the first time you fire but do you then put your arm around him and cry "Xavier speak to me what have I done?"
> No you aim a second shot into his back do your nerves get the better of you?
> No you fire a final bullet at zero range into his ear
> And this Sophie Auzanneau and I'm appalled to have to say it to a young girl like you
> This is what you did and didn't do
>
> *(New French Plays, 4)*[7]

In his restatement of the facts it is clear to the audience that he is playing a double game: on the one hand, pretending to stick to the facts and nothing but the facts; on the other hand, implying premeditation.

The Presiding Judge is firm but sympathetic; he makes it clear to Sophie that he wishes to ensure that she has a fair trial and to understand the reasons for her actions. He silences those who wish to play up the sensational aspects of the case and repeatedly appeals for the proceedings to take place in a calm and dignified manner. He only allows his carefully objective manner to slip into sarcasm on one occasion, when he is evoking Sophie's liaison with a German officer during the occupation. In the aftermath of the war it is clear that judicial objectivity had its limits: the case of girls consorting with the Occupier was one of them. Maître Cancé, the defense lawyer, is more than fair to Sophie; in fact, he shows her considerable sympathy and espouses her cause with a good deal of passion. At first it seems as though he alone really understands her. But, as the trial progresses, the audience begins to realize that he finds her as elusive as do the other members of the court. His final speech in her defense presents her as someone who has been rendered proud and unforgiving by the evil influence of her family upbringing, an interpretation challenged by many of the intercalated scenes, which show her as quite a different sort of person: vulnerable, unstable, very unsure of herself, and prone to fits of depression. Maître Cancé's defense throughout the trial has not in fact begun to elucidate the truth of Sophie's behavior. Instead, it has simply provided the counterpart to the arguments brought forward by the prosecution: when the Public Prosecutor claims that she is a monster Cancé seeks not to deny this but, rather, to excuse and explain it; when Lubé claims that she killed out of deliberate vengeance and showed no regret whatsoever he attempts to demonstrate evidence of her contrition and even apologizes to the court on her behalf.

In other words, the trial proceeds under a momentum of its own, entirely untroubled by the fact that, manifestly, the truth of Sophie's actions escapes the court. Vinaver himself chose a theatrical term to describe this process: "The show that is put on for the public by the judiciary runs without hitch or reversal, with no incident, sealed off from reality" (*Théâtre I*, 30).[8] What he means by this is that the rhetoric of accusation and defense run their dialectical course without any necessity for drawing Sophie into the process. All that is necessary is the act of murder, the death.

There are other idioms that enter into dialogue, as it were, with the judicial language; they are those associated with the different groups or institutions to which Sophie had belonged before her crime: her parents; her student friends at the medical faculty; her landlady at her lodgings; the professor who seduces her; the German army doctor with whom she forms a romantic attachment; the gunsmith from whom she buys the pistol that will be the instrument of Xavier's death. Each of these characters or groups speaks a different language or idiom, and each of them makes an attempt to analyze Sophie, to explain her motives, or to account for what it is that makes her act. All these opinions are different, and, because of the way they are intercalated with the court trial, all contest the explanations, judgments, and opinions that are developed by members of the court. Her parents, for example, alternate between brutal sarcasm and fussy overprotectiveness. Her father speaks to her with abruptness and lack of feeling; since her affair with a German doctor during the occupation, when she was only sixteen, he refers to her as *la pute* (the whore). He makes it clear that he has low expectations of her and takes a fatalistic attitude toward life. Whether it is his sons, both killed during the war, or his garden, destroyed by a storm, he expects the worst. Her mother is the opposite: full of concern for Sophie but mostly at the level of whether she is eating enough. She talks only of day-to-day details, and, insofar as she considers Sophie's future, it is only in conventional terms, looking forward to the time when she decides to marry and settle down, etc. Sophie's relationship with her parents exhibits the classic generation gap: they have preestablished notions of how she will behave and develop, evident in their rigid "parental" language. Her attempts to appeal to them to understand her way of looking at the world are met by blank incomprehension.

Her relationships with the other students are more promising in this respect. With her emotional instability goes an appealing, rather mercurial quality that fascinates Xavier, the young medical student from a respectable background. At first it seems as though he will be able to supply the love and understanding that she so desperately craves. But, although he sees that she is in need of help, Xavier can only respond to her by treating her as a frightened creature in need of protection. He cannot enter into her world and fails to understand her anguish. She expresses their failure to connect in terms of language.

Do you love me? And do I love you?
Words that don't come neat in their little compartments

But go rolling rolling on

(New French Plays, 1989, 23)[9]

He quickly finds her unpredictability more frightening than appealing and rejects Sophie in favor of Francine, who is prepared to contem-
plate a conventional marriage, in which she will play the subservient role
of receptionist while he establishes his medical practice. Sophie is able to
command a degree of loyalty from friends of the same sex, as is demonstrated in her relationship with Claudette, but Claudette's language also
betrays her belief in the importance of settling down and being "reason-
able." The pressures on female students in France at this time are
clarified by the behavior of the other male students, friends of Xavier's,
who insist that Sophie is asking for a good beating, that deep down she
wants it. The rhetoric of male dominance in the sex war, which emerges
from the brief glimpses of male student society, is both chilling and
entirely convincing.

The gunsmith, in a scene reminiscent of *Woyzeck* (the scene in
which Woyzeck purchases a knife), surprises Sophie by talking about
his family and the history of his collection, instead of restricting his
remarks to the commercial transaction. The result is that she is thoroughly intimidated by him, especially when it appears she may not have
enough cash for the pistol, and he sarcastically advises her to try in the
toy shop for a water pistol. Colonna, the professor with whom she has a
brief affair, completely fails to understand her, but Dr. Schlessinger is a
different matter. Schlessinger and Sophie are brought together in the
first instance by shared concern for the sick and wounded in the military
hospital. Schlessinger is old enough to be her father, but, unlike her
father, is lavish with his praise for her qualities and does not oblige her
to conform to any stereotypes. But, of course, he cannot offer any
permanent solution to her emotional needs since he is already married,
and the disparity between them is too great for them to be able to settle
down together, as Schlessinger explains to her when, in desperation at
losing Xavier to Francine, Sophie goes to visit him six years after the
war.

I'm an old quack an old Boche unappetizing at that
And you're a splendid young woman of twenty-three
My kitten's grown into a tigress

(New French Plays, 20)[10]

Despite their differences, all these relationships have one thing in common, which is that all are, to some extent, power relationships. In none of them is Sophie able to take a dominant role. In her relationship with Xavier it is always he who has the upper hand: she is unable to assert her own needs, and the most she can do is, occasionally, laugh at him. As for her parents, with them she cannot escape the role of the unsatisfactory dependent female who was never as good as her two brothers who died in the war. With the professor she is no more than a sexual conquest, and with the gunsmith she is just a child. With Schlessinger she enjoys only the spurious independence that comes with her role as his "kitten" or his "tiger." The only person prepared to say a good word for her in court is her landlady, Mme Guibot, who, as the flashbacks show, has behaved toward her with sympathy unclouded by censoriousness. But for all her sympathy she does not understand Sophie any better than the other characters and is equally surprised at Sophie's inability to conform to normal expectations of how a student should live.

Vinaver's fragmentary technique of presenting the action in a continuous present works particularly well in this play, giving an intense impression of Sophie torn between the varying demands of her different "selves." The scenes from her life before the trial are highly condensed, and their order does not respect chronology, so that the audience has to piece together the different "stories" of her life in much the same way that one might do in getting to know someone in real life. The flashbacks are arranged so as to clarify her predicament as a woman growing up in a world where she is expected to conform to role models proposed by men. Her German lover, her teacher, her father, her student boyfriend, all in their different ways cast her in roles that condemn her to passivity, denying her any possibility of personal fulfillment. In this situation all she can do is struggle unsuccessfully to pull together her different selves into one coherent personality. She fails because she can only experience life as a sum of fragmented parts, each of them a failure, with no center to hold it together. The dramatic method perfectly expresses this, as Sophie is torn between answering the members of the court, her lover, her father, etc., all coming at her from different angles in the same space and at the same time. The outcome is that she fails to satisfy anyone with her answers because the court authorities fail to draw her into their linguistic field. She adopts none of the attitudes expected in such circumstances: she is neither contrite nor angry nor defiant; she simply appears untouched by the proceedings of the court. Vinaver commented that in most judicial situations the people on trial tend to mold themselves to the judicial processes. One can observe a repression of reality. The dominated one enters the game on terms dictated by the dominators. An apparent harmony prevails. In the case of Sophie this pseudo-fusion fails to take. She resists in a diffuse, passive manner. As a result of her failure to participate, the judicial machine, while it continues to function, does so without getting any grip on the case.[11] (*Théâtre I*, 30)

There are obvious similarities between Sophie and Camus's Meursault in his novel *L'Etranger* (1942). Both are victims of a legal process that functions according to its own logic, taking little account of the real needs of the character concerned. In both the lawyers attempt to draw the accused into the process, to get them to collaborate in the assembling of a case, the consideration of motives, etc., and in both they fail. Of course, the point of view presented in Camus's novel is different: being a first-person narrative, everything is seen from Meursault's point of view. For most of the second half of the book Meursault, like Sophie, does not really understand what is happening to him and fails to grasp the precise details of the legal process. But after he has been condemned to death he reaches a point where he is able to make a positive affirmation of the value he sees in life. The occasion is the visit of the chaplain, which sparks off a passionate outburst by Meursault in which he declares his certainty that his way of life was right and that he is more sure of himself than the chaplain will ever be. In *Portrait d'une femme* Sophie never achieves a similar point of self-confidence and the discovery of her own voice. More-over, since Vinaver gives her no passages of introspective monologue, she is seen only in relation to others. So, for example, we see her from the points of view of Xavier, of her parents, of her friend Claudette, of Mme Guibot, of Dr. Schlessinger, etc., and for each of these she is a different person.

Her failure to find a voice of her own is her tragedy, and, by present-ing her in this way, Vinaver has sought to remain faithful to his source; her situation as the accused becomes an image for her whole condition. As a woman growing up in the France of the 1940s, she is not permitted to live an independent life (as Meursault could), nor is she able to trans-form her fragmented experience of the world into a coherent voice. Never-theless, the similarities between the two stories are striking, even down to the detail of both Meursault and Sophie firing several shots. Vinaver has made no secret of the debt he owes to Camus nor of his admiration for *L'Etranger*. (Chap. 2 examined the links between *L'Etranger* and Vinaver's novel *L'Objecteur* of 1951.) In *Portrait d'une femme* we can see Vinaver returning to a preoccupation with the figure of *l'objecteur*, but this time in female form. Sophie's approach to the world has much in common with that of Meursault, the outsider, or with Vinaver's "objectors" Bême and Belair. Like them, she is not interested in following established patterns of career development but can easily become totally absorbed by something as unimportant and ordinary as a beach, a pebble, an orange, a cat, a pear tree.

To date this play has not received its first professional performance in France. Donald Watson's English translation was given a staged reading by the Royal Shakespeare Company as part of the First Covent Garden Festival in London in September 1990. The director was Di Trevis, and the role of Sophie was taken by Juliet Stevenson.

L'Emission de télévision

L'Emission de télévision was written in 1988 and shows Vinaver still inventing new solutions to dramaturgical problems, still creating plays that go to the heart of contemporary experience of life in France today. It introduces thematic material that is new to Vinaver's theater, especially the subject of a society dominated by television, and does so through a type of dramatic construction not used before. Its treatment of the theme of justice gives it a strong link with *Portrait d'une femme*, but it also suggests links with a number of Vinaver's other plays through a variety of themes all having to do with human beings' relationships to one another or to social institutions. There is a close link with *Les Voisins* in the treatment of the theme of friendship, or neighborliness, and the ease with which that relationship can turn into rivalry. There is also a link with *Par-dessus bord* and the plays of the 1970s in the theme of work, of the role it plays in our lives, and the way our perceptions of ourselves and of others are linked to our employment (or lack of it). In *L'Emission de télévision* Vinaver develops this theme by concentrating attention on the many different ways in which people relate to social institutions and the ways in which their lives are shaped by them. The play also deals with the role of spectacle in society, investigating the extent to which we experience the quality of our social life through images, representations, performances. It questions the way in which real-life experience is transformed so that it may be enjoyed as entertainment broadcast through the media. Finally, the play deploys a familiar battle of languages, or of discourse. As the different worlds of work, home, politics, love, marketing, religion, etc., are brought into conflict with one another, the audience experiences a clash of different speech idioms and sees how each of these implies a method of structuring reality, or a "worldview," and that these methods or viewpoints may be mutually incompatible.

The structural originality of the play is that, instead of creating a form of simultaneous dramatic present time, as he did in *Portrait d'une femme*, he employs a "before and after" structure, presenting scenes that take place alternately before and after a pivotal event, so as to achieve a similar stretching of present time. The play is made up of twenty short scenes, in which the threads of four distinct stories are woven together and their characters brought into conflict. Each story involves the relationship between a couple (or couples) that will change under the pressure of external events. At the center of the play are two middle-aged couples, M. and Mme Delile and M. and Mme Blache; they have known each other for thirty or forty years and their relationship has gone through a number of ups and downs. Their world is invaded by Adèle and Béatrice, a couple of television researchers, who are working on a program to be devoted to the problem of unemployment, especially long-term unemployment, and who are looking for suitable subjects. The third couple is formed by a judge and his secretary, and the fourth is Paul Delile (twenty-four-year-old son of M. and Mme Delile) and Jacky, a young woman journalist. The pivotal event, never shown on stage, but which gives the action a fixed reference point and a "suspense" interest, is the murder of M. Blache. Although it provides the unequivocal mainspring of the action (Blache is quite definitely dead), the motives for the murder become more and more open to doubt as the play progresses; by the end the question of the motive and identity of the criminal have ceased to be the sole focus of the audience's attention; we are more interested in seeing how the event has been "digested," passed through the system without causing any major disturbance. In fact, the most surprising thing to emerge concerning the murder is how little effect it ultimately has on the various chains of events, which, after a brief hesitation, continue as if it had hardly even happened.

The murder's pivotal function is chiefly apparent in the dramatic structure, since the first dozen scenes take place alternately after and before it, giving the audience a kind of three-dimensional view of the characters involved by showing them both in ignorance of the murder (just before it happens) and coping with their awareness of it (just afterward). The play opens in the office of the *juge d'instruction*. In the French "inquisitorial" system of justice the *juge d'instruction* conducts all the preliminary examinations of those suspected of a crime and can call in whatever witnesses he or she chooses before drawing up the initial dossier, which he or she forwards to the public prosecutor. The post of judge is regarded as a job like any other functionary of the state: it has its own training and career structure. If he or she succeeds in passing the qualifying exams rapidly, a judge may be given a first posting when still very young, and in recent years there have been a number of much publicized cases in which young judges have become carried away by the considerable powers at their command and have brought ridicule on themselves by behaving rather like some self-righteous sheriff in an old-fashioned Western. In Vinaver's play the young judge, with the quaintly historical name of Phélypeaux, has just taken up his first post in a provincial town somewhere on the Loire. His one ally is his secretary, though theirs is a complex relationship in which they do not always see eye to eye. She likes to recount to him her lurid dreams, which all concern the cases that they are investigating and through which, she believes, the identity of each criminal is revealed. She tries to "organize" him, and he pretends to dismiss her, while in fact relying on her a good deal—there is something conjugal about their relationship. Through it we see the expression of a favorite theme in Vinaver's work, the complex power structures of dependence or interdependence that are engendered by people working together for long periods in the same office.

The second scene, set before the murder has taken place, introduces the audience to the Delile couple and to the theme of work, or, rather, in this case unemployment. After thirty-two years spent working for the same firm, manufacturing stationery, Delile has lost his job and has been unemployed for the past four years. He has at last, however, found a new job at Bricomarket, one of the gigantic new do-it-yourself "hypermarkets," which became a feature of French life in the course of the 1980s. His work involves hovering helpfully in the aisles, ready to answer customers' queries. The scene evokes the agonies of unemployment in one's fifties, for both partners in the marriage, and explores the theme of personal worth viewed as a factor of success or failure in employment. In the course of the scene a secondary, linked theme emerges, that of friendship or rivalry mediated through employment. Delile has a friend who is his coworker in the engineering department of the stationery firm

Blache. Both lost their jobs at the same time, but Blache is more of a man of the world than Delile and has been more successful in finding work again. Delile, who has doubts about appearing on television, suggests (against the advice of his wife) that Blache would be a better bet for the program.

The scene is driven forward by the investigation of the two television researchers. Delile's experiences are brought out in response to their questions, as they try to decide whether he would be suitable to take part in the program. In the relationship between Adèle and Béatrice the friendship-versus-rivalry theme is further explored. The couple that they form is different in kind from either the married couples or the couple formed by Phélypeaux and his secretary. On the surface theirs is a relationship of equality and easy friendship, but, in fact, each is in competition with the other for the favors of Vincent Bonnemalle, the all-powerful television presenter, who is a household name and who heads the program.

Scene 3 jumps back to *after* the murder of Blache and shows the judge interrogating Delile and embarking on the process of building up his own picture of characters and events, very different from that of the television researchers, which, in turn, is different from that of the Deliles. This is followed by a scene *before* the murder, in which Adèle, going behind Béatrice's back, visits the Blache home to see if Blache would be a more suitable candidate for the program. This is again followed by a scene *after* the murder, where we are introduced to a fourth couple—Paul, the delinquent son of the Deliles, and Jacky, a young journalist determined to make her mark by getting a scoop on the murder story. Each of these couples has their own particular environment, and the scenes switch between them. The judge and his secretary are always seen in their office, the Deliles and the Blaches in their respective homes, Adèle and Béatrice in their hotel room (unless they are visiting other characters), and Paul and Jacky are seen either in Paul's rented room or in the bar that is his spiritual home.

In the scenes that follow we see the judge proceeding to interview the various characters to whom we have been introduced, beginning to develop his hypothesis, and taking down statements. This is where the theme of language, or discourse, is most clearly raised, though it is also present, in less clearly explicit ways, in other scenes. The audience witnesses the process whereby the statements of the different witnesses coagulate into the shape of official depositions. The judge has these typed out by his secretary and offers them for signature with the ritual formula: *reconnais-*

sez-vous là vos paroles? (Do you recognize these as your words?) Manifestly, they do not, but they can do nothing about it. In other scenes the same theme is suggested by the failure of characters to understand one another—for example, the discrepancy between the television researchers' vision of unemployment on the one hand and Delile's account of how it felt to him on the other.

The major theme of the play might be described as the process of how one makes sense of one's life when one has to "rehearse" it. If a television producer wants to make a program about your situation, how do you present it (or re-present it)? What is the difference between an event described to a lover and the same event described before a judge? The success of the play at this level depends largely on the skill of the playwright in capturing accurately, in his dialogue, the expressions that the audience will recognize as typical of each new combination of character and situation. Although it is constructed from commonplaces, this dialogue does not degenerate into "slice-of-life" naturalism because the audience sees each circumstance from different points of view, and so there is room for critical judgment to intervene. In the scenes between the television researchers and the couples (both Blache and Delile) Vinaver achieves a deeply ironic presentation of the difficulties involved in being true to one's experience when that experience is not only very painful but is also being manipulated by someone else to fit their interpretation of the overall situation. Delile feels obscurely that, if he consents to take part in the program, his own sense of his life will be falsified. Blache has no such qualms but welcomes the chance to play a part for the cameras. Both reactions provoke a profound, if rather disturbing, humor.

Against these differing reactions of the older generation is set the attitude of Paul, representative of the next generation, who can see only the hypocrisy of his elders and who rejects their way of life out of hand. Paul is not interested in presenting or re-presenting himself, nor does he wish to occupy a place in the accepted patterns of work or career. When he needs to point to something that expresses his own worth he takes Jacky to see some paintings of the circles of hell that he has done for the walls of a bar. Jacky tries to convince him that his sense of feeling marginal is because his real father is Blache and that he had an affair with his mother about the time of his birth. This leaves Paul in a state of emotional turmoil and prepares for the final scene, in which he claims to have killed Blache, though by this stage the audience is clear that it could equally well have been done by Delile, Mme Delile, Béatrice, or a complete stranger.

Paul's reactions express another of Vinaver's regular themes: that of belonging versus exclusion, which he calls the "inside/outside." Every single character in the play experiences a painful divide between the need to belong and the sense of being excluded. For Blache and Delile this expresses itself mainly at the level of work versus unemployment. For Adèle and Béatrice it emerges through personal suspicion and jealousy in their ostensibly friendly relationship; each one worries about whether the other is "in" with Vincent Bonnemalle. For the young judge there is the problem of not being stranded in the small town of Orléans and of making a career; for Jacky there is the desire to become accepted as a "real" journalist—for her this means getting a job in Paris. Most crucially, for Paul there is the question of which father he belongs to.

Two-thirds of the way through the play the alternation of before-the-murder and after-the-murder scenes gives way to a more concentrated time structure as the action comes to a head and scene follows scene very rapidly or scenes take place simultaneously. Each of the different stories reaches a crisis point, and each of these crises provokes or reinforces the others. Because of Blache's sudden death, Delile *has* to be the television company's choice; he hesitates. Meanwhile, the judge has become convinced of Delile's guilt. He is about to have him arrested but is confronted by Béatrice and Adèle, who threaten him with public humiliation on their program if he does not agree to put off the arrest until after the filming is completed. This is the moment chosen by Paul to claim that *he* is the criminal, perhaps in order to oblige Jacky, with whom he is infatuated. Meanwhile, Delile's wife has persuaded him to accept participation in the program, and the audience is left with the image of the Delile couple nervously preparing for the arrival of the film crew but not knowing whether the next person to call will be Adèle and Béatrice or the police.

The general conclusion to emerge from the play is the sense of how difficult it is in contemporary society for personal relationships to be free from outside manipulation or inner rivalry. The various pressures to which the different characters are subjected all tend to drive them apart, set them against one another, lead them to doubt their own worth and to be suspicious of their neighbors' motives. This is aggravated by the intervention of the structures and practices of the television industry. Television is not cast simplistically as the villain of the piece, but its working methods are subjected to close scrutiny. Running through the play like a leitmotif is a reflection on how no attempt to portray a life on television can avoid falsification, even when the programmers have the most disinterested motives. Moreover, since television is an industry with its own internal imperatives, the notion of a disinterested investigation is shown to be well-nigh impossible.

Vinaver presents the medium of television as a magnifying mirror of the dominant ideological pressures exerted on individuals in our society. The temptation to identify a person's worth with his or her career position is endorsed, even in a program that claims to be lamenting the evil of unemployment. The consequences of unemployment are examined (by the television researchers) only at the individual level; the wider industrial, political, or social causes of the evil find no place in their program. So what Vinaver gives us is no simple rant at the inhumanity of late capitalism, but his play demonstrates, in complex and realistic detail, those forces in our society that, in the name of an illusory liberty of choice, lead us into competitive or instrumental relationships with one another, even when all we want is to arrive at simple conviviality. The multiple perspectives on the various themes that are raised, and the failure to provide a "solution" to the question of who did the murder, mean that it is up to each member of the audience to make up his or her mind. But Vinaver's refusal to tie up the ends does not imply failure to confront the issues: on the contrary, the play shows how value judgments are an unavoidable part of daily life, without letting us forget that they are also, unavoidably, partial.

The play received its first production at the Odéon in Paris in January 1990, where it played for six weeks before going on to the Théâtre National de Strasbourg. It was directed by Jacques Lassalle and designed by Yannis Kokkos; the strong cast of actors were all members of the Comédie Française company. Lassalle was sensitive to the playwright's desire for the minimum of gaps between the scenes and agreed with him that the transitions between each of the twenty scenes should be almost like cinematic cuts. But, instead of following the stage directions and achieving this by performing the play with a minimal set, he wanted to achieve an effect more like a lap dissolve than a cut. He also felt that the particular environment in which the different scenes take place (the Deliles's kitchen, the Blache's living room, the judge's office, the researchers' hotel room, etc.) needed to be shown in concrete detail. So Kokkos designed a complicated set, with separate structures for each of the different rooms and a mechanism that allowed each of them in turn to slide noiselessly onstage at the same time as its predecessor was gliding off. Although this did not entirely avoid the difficulty that Vinaver and

Françon had encountered with *L'Ordinaire*—of imposing an excessively naturalistic performance style—the almost magical swiftness of the changes and the fact that they took place in full view of the audience certainly achieved the effect desired by Lassalle, as if one were flicking from one channel to another on a television screen. The only serious loss was in the last scene (20), for which Vinaver had specified that the Delile kitchen and the judge's office simultaneously be overlapping on stage. Given the rigidity of the structures that had been built for these two rooms, it was impossible to get them to overlap, and so the two parts of scene 20 had to be separated out and played one after the other, thus destroying the effect of counterpoint as the Delile couple rehearses for the television broadcast at the same time as the judge is fighting with Adèle and Béatrice about whether it can happen at all.

The production was notable for some superb performances, especially that of Alain Pralon as Delile. In this production Delile emerged as the still center of the play: whereas every other character was obsessed with the need to get ahead in their careers, Delile alone maintained a certain detachment. Some of the time it seemed as though he was not so much detached as lost. But, even at his most pathetic, waving his damaged finger (wounded when demonstrating an electric saw to a customer at Bricomarket), he retained a certain integrity, a fundamental passive resistance to the positions into which other people kept trying to push him. It was clear that he was a close cousin of Bême, Belair, and Sophie Auzanneau, the objectors who, against all the odds, manage to preserve a kind of innocence.

The play received its English-language premiere at the Gate Theatre, London, in 1992. The production was by Kim Dambaek, and it earned the author's approval by its use of minimal settings and by overlapping all the scenes on the same stage area, as specified in the stage directions. The reaction of the London critics was largely favorable, but the minuscule size of the theater (thirty seats) prevented this powerful production from having the same impact as the French premiere.

NOTES

1. Le théâtre de Vinaver constitue une sorte de répertoire de la francité. Des événements, des objets, des manières de parler sont prélevés dans le paysage de la France pour être tissés dans la trame des pièces qui forment une sorte de musée d'ethnographie française et contemporaine. Le chômage des cadres, le cinéma

tchèque, les grandes surfaces, la pilule, les happenings, la loterie nationale, la pollution . . . toute une série d'objets qui n'ont pas pour destination de former un "décor," ils sont la matière même des pièces et non des images. Ce qui tombe sous le sens devient ainsi étrange. Il reste un peu d'air autour de ces objets, ils ne sont pas refondus, ils gardent leur fraîcheur et avouent leur terroir. La drôlerie des pièces de Vinaver vient certainement de cette manière d'accrocher les objets et les faits et c'est par là qu'il est assurément cousin de Tati. Si les personnages des films de Tati se mettaient à parler, ils le feraient comme ceux de Vina, appelons-le ainsi le temps d'un paragraphe.

2. Ce quelque chose qu'Erdman sait faire et que je ne sais pas faire et après quoi je cours: l'extrême grossissement du trait.

3. On y discute beaucoup, et les idées dont il est débattu ne sont plus d'actualité pour nous. Mais le *traitement* apporté par Gorki à ces débats, ainsi qu'aux situations et actions qui accompagnent ces débats, traitement contrapuntique et fondé sur le principe du thème et de la variation, de l'entrecroisement des thèmes et de leurs variations, engendre une matière d'une richesse sans limites dans ses résonances.

4. De ce fabliau, qu'on dirait inspiré de Labiche, Vinaver a tiré un bizarre vaudeville contemporain, acide, dérangeant, très subtil et follement drôle.

5. En effet, s'il est vrai que ces cinq pièces se concentrent chacune sur le mouvement interne qui agite une cellule (familiale ou professionnelle), il n'en reste pas moins que leur visée ne diffère pas fondamentalement de celle des pièces symphoniques: faire apparaître la porosité entre le noyau intime de la vie et les grandes pulsations du monde auquel ce noyau participe.

6. Mesquinerie peut-être mais moi je m'intéresse aux faits
Je m'en tiens aux faits

7. Oui vous tirez une première fois il s'écroule mais alors le prenez-vous par les épaules pour crier "Xavier réponds-moi qu'ai-je fait?"
Non vous tirez une deuxième fois dans le dos allez-vous avoir une crise de nerfs?
Non vous tirez une dernière balle dans l'oreille à bout touchant
Voilà Sophie Auzanneau et j'ai l'épouvante de la dire à une jeune femme comme vous
Voilà ce que vous avez fait et ce que vous n'avez pas fait

8. Le spectacle que met en scène la Justice se déroule sans accident ni péripétie, sans événement, étanche an réel.

9. Tu m'aimes? Et moi je t'aime?
Des mots qui n'arrivent pas dans leurs petites cases
Qui roulent qui roulent

10. Je suis un vieux toubib bohe vieux et pas appétissant
Toi tu es une jeune femme de vingt-trois ans jeune splendide
Mon chaton est devenu un tigre

11. Dans la plupart des situations de justice, les justiciables tendent à se mouler aux formes de la Justice. On assiste à un refoulement du réel. Le dominé entre dans le jeu du dominant. Une apparente harmonie prévaut.
Avec Sophie, cette pseudo-fusion ne réussit pas à se faire. Elle est réfractaire de façon diffuse, passive. Du fait de ce défaut d'adhésion de sa part, la machine judiciaire, sans s'arrêter de tourner, tourne à vide.

Chapter 7

Vinaver Now

At the beginning of the 1990s Vinaver's creative drive appears to be as strong as ever. He has reached the height of his profession and holds an undisputed place as France's leading active playwright. He has had the satisfaction of seeing his complete plays collected and published in two volumes—an honor granted to no other living playwright in France in the past decade—and is regularly invited to make pronouncements on the state of French play writing today. He has successfully negotiated the transition from the world of business and commerce to the life of the professional writer, dividing his time between creative and teaching work. One of his greatest triumphs is to have succeeded in introducing creative theater writing classes into the purist Parisian academic establishment. And yet, despite these outstanding achievements, his name is not yet widely known in France: he has not been granted the recognition awarded to the leading dramatists of the previous generation such as Camus, Sartre, Beckett, Ionesco, and Genet. Setting aesthetic value judgments temporarily aside, it is instructive to consider some of the factors in Vinaver's career and in the current state of French theater that might go to explain his role and place in that theater today.

The most notable gap in Vinaver's career is the absence of a major "hit." Although his recent plays have been successful with critics and public alike, neither *Les Voisins* nor *L'Emission de télévision* enjoyed a long run. Part of the explanation for this is to be found in the state of French theater funding: institutions such as the Odéon and the Théâtre National de Strasbourg, which coproduced *L'Emission de télévision*, receive sufficient funds from the Ministry of Culture to not need to rely on transfers to the commercial sector. Such transfers, which are common in the London theater, are unknown in Paris. From the point of view of the theater companies this is an advantage, since it means that they can count on working together for the whole season and avoid the repeated disruption that is caused whenever the cast of a successful production is seduced away by the chance of a long run in a commercial theater. But, although it creates good conditions for companies to work in, this state of affairs is bad for the author. It means that, once the planned performances of his work are complete, there is very little likelihood of the play, however successful, continuing to run for a longer period. Moreover, the rivalry between companies and directors is such that, once a play has been successfully premiered by one director, its chances of a second production are quite small. This is a feature of the last twenty-five years; it was not the case in the 1950s, when Planchon's production of *Les Coréens* was followed, six months later, by Serreau's in Paris (and was to have been followed by Monnet's the following summer if it had not been banned). But by the time of *Par-dessus bord* things had changed, and Vinaver discovered, to his chagrin, that once Planchon had produced his version no other director was willing to risk comparisons. Vinaver had to wait another ten years before seeing the second production of the play by Charles Joris.

Par-dessus bord came at a bad time for French play writing in general. After the upheavals of 1968 many of the most dynamic French theater companies dispensed with the playwright altogether, preferring to devise their own material, a process that became known as *la création collective* (see Bradby, *Modern French Drama, 1940–1990*, 191–226). An important side effect of this newfound trend for devised plays was to increase the power and authority of the director, since he (almost all were men, with the honorable exception of Ariane Mnouchkine) found himself in overall control of the devising process. In the course of the 1970s directors in France consolidated their claim to being the main creative force at work on the modern stage by developing a theater of dazzling visual complexity. The major successes of the period were almost all productions in which the written text was an unimportant or malleable element, as evidenced in the work of Planchon, Mnouchkine, Wilson, etc. (see Bradby and Williams, *Director's Theatre*). Vinaver's work, with its emphasis on text, was swimming against a powerful tide.

Of the few new playwrights who did emerge in the course of the 1970s almost all had served their apprenticeships as members of a theater company, like Jean-Claude Grumberg, who had been an actor for many years before he began to write, or Michel Deutsch, who had started out working as a dramaturge for the Théâtre National de Strasbourg. This route into the play-writing profession was largely beneficial in that it provided the French theater with craftsmen who had a thorough grounding in the practicalities of writing for performance. But for Vinaver, who found himself bracketed by critics with this young generation of writers, it was not helpful to have to confront the new orthodoxy among theater people, an orthodoxy that held that the only way to become a good playwright was to have practical experience in a theater. Not only had Vinaver never worked in a theater; he had always made a point of defending the autonomy of the play text as well. In his remarks on his own work, prepared for submission to the university when he was seeking professorial status in 1986, he insisted on the absence of any difference *in kind* between the creation of a play text and the creation of other literary forms (poems, novels, essays): "the process of writing a play is no different from that involved in any poetic production." The difference, he argued, comes afterward and "has to do with incarnation, demanding the actor's voice and gesture—a physical exchange with an audience" (*Mémoire sur mes travaux*, 38–39).

The processes of play writing and play production are, thus, in Vinaver's view, two quite separate activities. He has only once been tempted to participate in the production process (directing aspects of *L'Or-dinaire*) and prefers to retain a certain distance: "The theater has everything to gain from being based on texts that resist it, that put up a resistance notably to the actor and to the director—texts that are 'insoluble,' as Antoine Vitez has said—and the emergence of such texts cannot be fostered by having the author participate in the practical work of staging" (*Mémoire sur mes travaux*, 60).[1] This is such an unusual position to take up in the practice of French theater today that it borders on eccentricity. Most playwrights are extremely keen to participate in rehearsals of their own work; they see this as a way of retaining power over it and of preventing some of the worst excesses to which all-powerful directors are prone. Vinaver, on the other hand, feels that the logic of his insistence on the autonomy of the text requires that the author retire when the process of staging begins, hoping that his work will find sympathetic and imaginative interpreters. He has not hesitated to condemn those whom he considers to have used or distorted his work for their own purposes and has been lavish in praise of those directors who productions have been faithful to the texts, notably Charles Joris of the Théâtre Populaire Romand at La Chaux-de-Fonds in Switzerland and Sam Walters of the Orange Tree

Theatre, Richmond (London). He has been outspoken in his criticism of the whole system of lavishly state-funded theater in France, which he believes has a counterproductive effect on playwrights.

In 1991 he published a long essay in *New Theatre Quarterly,* "Decentralization as Chiaroscuro," in which he examined the history of the growth of support for the theater by the French state since the war and came to some outspoken conclusions about the system's current failures. He argued that, despite the increasing sums of money devoted to the theater sector in the course of the 1980s, the French theater establishment has lost its sense of direction. In the first decades after the war the pioneers of the decentralization movement, such as Dasté, Sarrazin, Planchon, and Vilar, among many others, were driven by a mission founded on an idea of universal significance: "The idea was that theatre is tantamount to a human right: that its function is to bring people together and elevate their minds at the same time as it brings them pleasure. Hence its legitimacy. Hence the basic tenet that theatre activity should not be required to pay for itself, but that it should be construed as a public service" (70).

This grand mission, which united the early pioneers, evaporated in the course of the 1960s and 1970s, as their broad humanist belief in universal values was questioned by the younger, politically radical generation and as it became apparent that the idea of building up a mass working-class audience for the theater was a utopian dream. But the fundamental irony identified by Vinaver is that, despite the evaporation of the missionary certainties, the organizational and financial structures of decentralization have continued to be expanded and consolidated. This process has produced a lavishly funded state apparatus run by powerful theater directors who no longer feel the need to justify their position by reference to the old aims. So what is it, asks Vinaver, that motivates them? His reply is that they are driven by the "logic of difference": "The logic whereby a director is compelled, as it were, to show himself as being extraordinary, in order to justify the extraordinary amount of money he requires and in order to obtain even more, which will allow him to mount things even more different and more extraordinary, and so on *ad infinitum*" ("Decentralization," 72). He suggested that there are a dozen or so directors in what he called the "Big League" who are caught in this trap and showed that their extravagances are eating up an increasingly large proportion of the state's theater spending, with the result that there is a growing gap between the funds they receive and those allotted to smaller companies. He concluded that the whole system is suffering from a kind of institutional sclerosis in which the narcissism of big-spending directors is driving out both the playwrights and the public: "something in the nature of *perestroika* is called for" (76). Attacks of this kind clearly do not endear him to the directors concerned, and they strengthen the impression he sometimes gives of being an outsider on the fringes of the French theater establishment.

But Vinaver's independence and willingness to criticize have not, in fact, damaged his standing. There is no other contemporary playwright whose work has been so regularly produced by the very directors of the Big League whom he singles out for criticism. The current director of the Comédie Française, Jacques Lassalle, has directed the premieres of four of his plays; his predecessor, Antoine Vitez, directed the first production of *Iphigénie Hôtel* and supported Vinaver's work in various ways, including the commissioning of a one-act play, *Le Dernier sursaut*. Moreover, Vinaver's standing with the officials of the Ministry of Culture could not be higher; in 1982, when the decision was taken to set up a separate theater committee within the Centre National des Lettres, he was invited by Jack Lang (minister of culture) to be its first chairman, a post he held for a five-year term, from 1982 to 1986. During this period he compiled a major report about the causes of the weak state of theater publishing at the time, which concluded with a thirty-seven point list of recommendations for action to bring about an improvement.

The report was based on a very far-reaching inquiry, in the course of which advice was sought from publishers, bookshops, distributors, the media, authors, dramatists, theatergoers, critics, educators, etc. The complete text of the report runs to 136 pages and exhibits the same thoroughness and respect for detail that characterizes all of Vinaver's work. It suggests that no single factor can be held accountable for the crisis in theater publishing; rather, it results from a combination of changes that have taken place—in theater practice, in the marketing of books, in the way that playwrights are viewed by the media, by the educational establishment, and by themselves. It also has to do with the antiquated practices of the Société des Auteurs et Compositeurs Dramatiques (S.A.C.D), set up by Beaumarchais in the eighteenth century and still the sole agency representing the commercial interests of French playwrights. As a result of the recommendations of the committee presided over by Vinaver, there has been a rapid improvement in theater publishing in France. The publishing house Actes Sud has built up a very large list of theater works, including those of many new playwrights, and other publishers have begun to bring out play texts as well. Reforms have been introduced into the S.A.C.D. A major history of theater in France (edited by J. Jomarron) and an encyclopedia of theater (edited by M. Corvin) have both been published in recent years (1989 and 1991, respectively), as recommended, with financial assistance from the Centre National des Lettres. Most important of all for the long term were the committee's recommendations for educationists to pay more attention to the theater; a recent agreement between the ministries of culture and education promises to enlarge the scope of theater education in schools and universities.

If Vinaver is seen today as the leader of a new and more militant generation of playwrights, it is also because of a third area of innovation, which has had as much influence among his peers as the success of his own plays and of his committee work. This is his pioneering work in the teaching of creative writing. French universities have been slow to develop drama departments in which creative work is recognized as being as important as academic or theoretical work. His first teaching appointment was in 1982, when he was invited by Bernard Dort to join the Institut d'Etudes Théâtrales of Paris III (Sorbonne) as associate professor and elected to take a class in practical criticism. Two years later he proposed a creative writing class, entitled *Atelier d'écriture théâtrale,* which ran for three years (1984–87); since then he has been teaching similar classes at the theater department of Paris VIII (Saint Denis). At the end of his first *atelier* (workshop) at Paris III Vinaver decided to issue typescripts of the twenty plays that had been written by students and to circulate them among interested people. This had a considerable influence, and other playwrights began to look for ways in which they could conduct similar classes. In 1989 money was made available by a group of sponsors, including the ministries of culture and education, the S.A.C.D., and the Centre National des Lettres, for thirteen playwrights to go into schools and colleges to conduct classes on aspects of play writing. The report of this experiment, "L'Apprenti auteur dramatique," in *Théâtre/Public* includes a long analysis of Vinaver's original class of 1984–85, demonstrating its seminal effect on the development of this kind of teaching in France.

But it is as a playwright that Vinaver would principally wish to be judged. Near the outset of his career, in his article on *The Shoemaker's Holiday* (*Ecrits sur le théâtre,* 175–77), Vinaver called for a redefinition of the playwright's art and of its function in society. It is fair to ask how far he has succeeded, in the course of a dozen major plays and four adaptations, in meeting this aim. A brief reminder of the state of French theater at the end of the 1950s (when that article appeared) will help in answering this question. The French theater of that time was responding to the violent political upheavals in which the Fourth Republic collapsed by polarizing into violently opposed camps. On the one hand were the champions of the New theater (recently dubbed "Theater of the Absurd" by Esslin in his book of 1961) led by Ionesco. On the other was the new political theater, modeling itself on Brecht, whose spokesmen were Adamov, Planchon, and the editorial team of *Théâtre Populaire*. Both of these polarized camps were suspicious of the high-flown humanist mission of the decentralized theaters. If they agreed on anything, it was that heroic drama and noble sentiment were irrelevant to the new generation living with the consequences of the cold war and the threat of nuclear destruction. In these circumstances any new young playwright with an ambition to write about contemporary reality found himself under pressure to enroll in one or another of the two camps. It may be that the "writer's block" experienced by Vinaver in the decade from 1959 to 1969 was due as much to these pressures as to the demands of his employer, Gillette.

It is in this context that *Par-dessus bord* emerges as a major turning point in the postwar French theater. The play is both manifesto and demonstration—"*défense et illustration*"—for a new style of dramatic writing that can cut a path through the impasse of the old binary oppositions (*either* political *or* absurdist). In this monster of a play he found a way to bring together political discussion *and* black comedy; accurate depiction of economics *and* experiments in dramatic form; the banalities of everyday experience *and* surreal happenings; accurate depiction of reality *and* heightened theatricality; verbal drama *and* the drama of bodies in space. More important, he did not just bring them together but also made of their juxtaposition the very substance of the play's dramatic movement. This was highly original at the time, and the plays Vinaver has written in the course of the following two decades have shown that it was no isolated phenomenon but truly the foundation of a new approach to dramaturgical problems. In this and in succeeding plays he has risen to the challenge he set himself: that of "transforming the most uninteresting raw material into an object of enjoyment and knowledge" (*Ecrits sur le théâtre*, 132).

Part of his success must be attributed to his erudition and to the enormous range of material that he is able to draw on. In his work echoes can be found of every stage in the European theater tradition, from ancient Greece to the modern world. But it is precisely because of the multiplicity of these borrowings that he is able to remold them into his own, unmistakably personal style. Rather than become fixated on a particular author, he is always looking for alternatives and counterweights: in ancient Greece he draws on not only the Homeric but also the Hesiodic, not only the Sophoclean but also the Aristophanic worldviews. From the Elizabethan period he has adapted not only Dekker's domestic *Shoemaker's Holiday* but also Shakespeare's *Julius Caesar*. In the modern period he has expressed his admiration for Chekhov and Gorky but has also written on Jarry and Strindberg and adapted *The Suicide* by Erdman. Most characteristic of all was his highly original article on the relationship between Stanislavsky and Brecht, written at a time when it was generally assumed that these two directors had nothing in common.

His views on ancient Greek drama were influenced by the now outmoded anthropological school of critics, but his manner of digesting their theories has enabled him to distill certain fundamental elements of theater that have proved highly productive in his own work. A case in point is his repeated affirmation that the most powerful theater always involves a rite of passage, in which a group of people moves from one state to another and is changed in the process. His evidence for this belief is not confined to ancient Greek theater: he finds it to be just as true, for example, of Strindberg's late plays. More important, this insight is made to fuel his own writing: every one of his plays charts a dynamic process in which people are changed. From Belair in *Les Coréens,* who loses contact with his old companions but gains insight into a new cultural order, to the executives of Housies confronting their own mortality in *L'Ordinaire*, this is a constant factor in all of Vinaver's plays. It is made all the more powerful by the playwright's ability to shadow present realities with mythical archetypes in such a way that even the most ordinary situations resonate with other associations. The only contemporary French dramatist to achieve a comparable effect is Bernard-Marie Koltès.

Like Koltès, Vinaver stands out among contemporary playwrights for his determination to reflect something of the nation's social and political life without abandoning dramaturgical experiment. By taking on the large themes, such as justice, the role of television and the media, the effects of big business on the lives of ordinary people, etc., he has accepted the traditional responsibility of the playwright, not only to express his own inner voice but also to reflect the social fabric of which he is a part. And yet, by clinging to his early conviction that theater "is not a proposition but a revelation," he has avoided falling into the trap of well-meaning didactic theater: "It [theater] does not present itself as a collection of problems to be resolved but as a configuration of signs establishing their own reality. Its purpose is not to demonstrate how the world is made but to represent the world in its immediacy" (*Ecrits sur le théâtre*, 25–26).[2] The great strength of Vinaver's theater, and the quality that gives it universal appeal, is its ability to capture, and to represent through its dialogue, a reality that we all recognize. Its distinction is that it is not content to rest there but, instead, constantly re-presents this reality from different viewpoints, so that the plays are at one and the same time a representation of the world that carries immediate conviction and a questioning of the very methods of representation that are being employed.

Because of this, critics have always had difficulty in defining precisely the relationship of Vinaver's drama to established forms of realism or naturalism. They have found it difficult to reconcile the veracity and truth-to-life of the situations and characters he creates with the fragmentary, experimental nature of his dramatic construction. An adequate critical account needs to do justice to both these things. It must come to terms with the idea of a theater that is *descriptive,* in the sense of the word employed by Vinaver when writing about *Troilus and Cressida* ("a rigorously descriptive theater" whose function is to reveal) but also analytical in the way it fragments its subject matter, denying the possibility of a single, unproblematic perspective, abandoning a theater of linear narrative for one of multiple viewpoints.

The critic who has best expressed the relationship of Vinaver's work to reality is Roland Barthes in his essay on *Les Coréens.* Had he survived, he might have refined his definition in the light of Vinaver's work in the 1980s, but his account still has relevance, especially paragraph 3, in which he posits the need for the invention of "a new language" (*un langage nouveau*):

> This must be understood in its fullest sense as a discovery and conversion of the word, leading to a new *usage* of reality. [A footnote adds: *Usage* must be understood in the Brechtian sense of "custom": "What I need is a new Great Custom to be introduced at once, to wit the custom of rethinking every new situation" (*He Who Says No,* 79).] Such a conversion need not exclude politics in its fullest sense. An example could be seen in the conversion of "language" brought about recently between the Russia of Stalin and that of Kruschev, and

which we can see today affects *the whole* of reality. *Mutatis mutandis, Aujourd'hui* tries out a language of consent, one might call it *coexistence* in other quarters, not taking the word in the restricted way it is used in international politics, but in the general sense of: a jettisoning of "resentment," a *correction* in the recognition of the *immediate* quality of reality (*Aujourd'hui*, as its title indicates, places present time before us as matter that is susceptible to *immediate* structuring and contradicts the traditional dogma of revolution as an essentially eschatalogical time scale). (*Théâtre I,* 38)[3]

Barthes is here explaining how the refusal to filter experience through established systems of interpretation, insisting on its *immediacy,* opens up new possibilities. It is a theme that he had already developed in relation to Camus's *L'Etranger* (a work whose importance for the young Vinaver has already been mentioned), when he described it as achieving "an innocent style" (un style innocent). He went on to explain that "the exercise of a language (and objectively literature is nothing other than a language) inevitably leads to automatism, repetition, themes within which innocence is no longer possible" (*Combat,* 1 August 1947). It is because Vinaver has consistently retained this "innocence" in his presentation of reality that his plays have retained what Cournot, reviewing *Les Travaux et les jours,* described as the impression "that life itself seems to be captured in the fullness of its flux and mystery" (see chap. 4).

It is in *Par-dessus bord* and the subsequent chamber plays that we have seen Vinaver struggling with ways of preserving this "innocence" while *also* achieving ironic distance from his subject matter, and this can explain why the fragmentary, contrapuntal method reaches its most extreme form in *La Demande d'emploi.* Vinaver needed to invent a dramatic structure that would stretch the experience of the present moment, rendering it with maximum vividness, without condemning his readers/audience to be locked into that one moment, placing blinkers on them, as it were, so that they could see no alternatives. The dramaturgical solution was the kaleidoscopic method of fragmentary experiences constantly re-presented from differing perspectives. This preserved the vivid realism of the lived experience while at the same time detaching the spectator from becoming trapped in a single perspective on the situation with no alternatives offered. On the contrary, it enabled each perspective or presentation to challenge all the others and thus opened the way to a complex response. The quality he was aiming for was the one he identified in his review of

Troilus and Cressida, when he spoke of *cette absolue plénitude de l'instant présent* (this absolute fullness of the present moment) (*Ecrits sur le théâtre,* 97).

The dramaturgical and literary methods developed by Vinaver to achieve this result are both personal and highly original, although he draws inspiration from a wide variety of sources, as we have seen. As if he were afraid to destroy them by too much analysis, Vinaver is wary of explaining his methods. When he does so he often employs terms borrowed from the scientific vocabulary, as if to emphasize the fact that the creative process is not entirely within his control but is something he observes, trying to understand it and to channel it, as a scientist does with natural phenomena. In this respect he resembles Nathalie Sarraute, who in 1939 borrowed the term *tropismes* from the vocabulary of the biological sciences to convey imprecise feelings or emotional impulses that precede linguistic expression but which may give rise to it. Sarraute's own definition of the term *tropismes* is as follows: "They are indefinable movements that slip very rapidly at the limits of our consciousness; they are at the origin of our gestures, of our words and of the emotions that we show, that we believe we feel, and that we are incapable of defining. They seem to me to constitute the secret source of our existence" (preface to *L'Ere du Soupçon* [1964], 8).[4]

Sarraute's short stories, in the volume entitled *Tropismes,* show people reacting to one another or to outside stimuli with psychological or physical impulses of which they are only partly conscious. The stories do not generally contain much action: they are mood studies of what she calls "interior dramas made up of attacks, triumphs, retreats, defeats, caresses, bites, rapes, murders, generous renunciations, or humble submissions" (*L'Ere du Soupçon* [1956], 99). Vinaver's work starts from a strictly comparable investigation of what he calls "impulses" (*poussées*) but which could equally well be defined as "tropisms." But he takes the process further. He shows the interior dramas, of which Sarraute speaks, emerging sufficiently into the open to come into conflict with other such interior dramas. Moreover, he shows how many of these impulses are specifically linguistic in origin and that the linguistic form they take will often determine the whole manner in which a person relates to the world outside. Where Sarraute dwells obsessively on the initial impulse, Vinaver builds and develops, constructing chains of such impulses, showing how they interweave to create the texture of everyday life.

For Vinaver to achieve such an accurate pinpointing of the linguistic *poussée,* or tropism, he had to be obsessed with common usage, with the way keywords will dominate and color people's speech, with the whole mass of idiomatic turns of phrase that go to make up the linguistic texture of our everyday reality as we articulate it to one another and to ourselves. Evidence of this obsessive observation exists in the form of a book entitled *Les Français vus par les français.* The author, Guy Nevers, is a pseudonym for Michel Vinaver, but his role in this book is more that of compiler than author. The book is the fruit of a concentrated period of brainstorming, during which a dozen people, all strangers to one another, came together to voice their feelings, ideas, convictions, uncertainties, and dreams of what it meant to be French. The method employed was to table a question—for example, "What does it mean to me to be French?"—then to encourage the participants to say whatever came into their heads. The results of two days of concentrated talking were taped and analyzed by Vinaver, who grouped the results together under fifty-two different headings, each broken up into clusters of keywords or ideas, with a commentary on the group image that emerged from them. The idea was to provide a lighthearted self-portrait of a nation; humorous line drawings were added, and the book was marketed as having universal interest. In reality it is extremely monotonous to read because it catalogs all the building blocks needed to construct a national self-portrait and stops there. But, as an indication of how a playwright works, it is very revealing. It shows an encyclopedic interest in the words people use and a patient willingness to classify and establish connections between classifications. It reminds one of Flaubert's *Dictionnaire des idées reçues* and reveals the painstaking work that is necessary if a writer is to achieve the sensitivity to word and idiom and to varieties of characteristic usage that we have found in Vinaver's plays.

In summing up the achievement of Vinaver the playwright one is drawn back once again to the comparison with his acknowledged model, T.S. Eliot. The features that he picks out to characterize *The Waste Land* can equally well be applied to his own plays:

> The primacy of rhythm out of which comes an impulse toward meaning [*une poussée ver le sens*]; the contrapuntal treatment of a multiplicity of autonomous themes; the preeminence of themes over elements of plot; the movement given to the themes so that they collide or scrape up against one another, even reaching the point of fusion, rather than a movement of causal links; the precedence of the word,

characters only constructing themselves in the wake of an eruption
of verbal material; the emergence, by trial and error, of a structure
discovering itself, rather than the imposition of an existing framework (subject, situation, characters); the molecular level at which an
articulation is formed between the most universal and the most trivial,
between the mythic and the everyday, between what is most ancient
and what is absolutely contemporary. . . the practice of joining, of
collage, of shredding; also poverty of language, the renunciation of
fine rhetoric and ornament. (*La Terre vague*, 4)[5]

This describes well the original approach to play writing that Vinaver's
work successfully exemplifies. It omits only the peculiarly vivid representation of present time, and here his natural point of comparison is with
painting rather than with poetry, since painting is an art form that does
not employ time sequentially. Rauschenberg, a painter much admired by
Vinaver, was reported in the French journal *Arts* as saying: "I am in the
present. I seek to celebrate the present within my own limitations but
using all my resources." In his pictures he brought together fragmentary
images of widely differing provenance, explaining: "Painting is part of
both art and life. Neither one nor the other can be depicted. I try to work
in the breach between the two" (*Arts*, 821, 10 May 1961), which reminds
us of the quotation from Braque about painting the "in-between," which
Vinaver placed at the head of *Iphigénie Hôtel*. In this respect his work
suggests affinities not only with Eliot but with David Jones, especially his
monumental First World War novel, *In Parenthesis*.

The salient defining features of Vinaver's work are thus broadly
Modernist; aesthetically, they are concerned with the same problems as
were Eliot, Joyce, the Cubist painters, and the Surrealist poets. But, as a
postwar writer, he looks for inspiration to contemporary artists or writers
such as Rauschenberg, Camus, Borges, and Godard. His determination
to find ways of representing contemporary reality fuels the radical experimentation that is so much a feature of his work and anchors it firmly
within its own time. Moreover, as one might expect from a friend of
Roland Barthes, his work is especially rich in its exploitation of intertextu-
ality and displays many of the preoccupations most fundamental to postmodernism. Chief among these is its use of interruption, discontinuity,
and irony. One of the most typical features of postmodernist writing is its
tendency to intercut one kind of discourse with another. But, although
this technique has been widely practiced in prose writing, Vinaver is the

first person to have systematically explored its implications for dramatic writing, beginning with *Par-dessus bord* at the end of the 1960s. Out of this experimentation came the characteristic tone of his plays, both critical of, and in complicity with, the dominant discourses of his society (see Hutcheon, *A Poetics of Postmodernism*, 222). His presentation of characters who are "à la fois broyé par un système et en complète communion avec lui" (both crushed by a system and in complete communion with it) (*Ecrits sur le théâtre*, 286) is made possible by a very postmodern play of irony, switching repeatedly from the inside view of a given situation or discourse to the outside view and back again.

Many other elements of Vinaver's work might be cited as typically postmodern, but most predate the invention of the term *postmodernism*. His insistence on the nondidactic nature of theater (dating back to 1955) and his discovery of how a play can *both* create its own reality *and* proceed to challenge that reality, a discovery that he attributes to his first encounter with *Ubu Roi*, could be seen as profoundly postmodernist *avant la lettre* (before the term was coined). The same is true of his emphasis on dehierarchization of everyday experience. As we have seen, this has its origin in Camus's particular brand of Existentialist thought and in what Barthes described as "writing degree zero," or an "innocent style." It lies at the very foundation of Vinaver's first play (written in 1955), and the idea was expressed in theoretical terms when he was embroiled in the difficulties over *The Shoemaker's Holiday* (1959). Two decades later he expressed this notion again, in impeccably postmodern style, in an article dated 1980 that consisted of an alphabetical list of twenty-one headings designed to define "*une écriture du quotidien*" (see *Ecrits sur le théâtre*, 126–34). The last heading in the list is "Hierarchy" and begins as follows:

In response to social pressures we are constantly in the process of "hierarchizing." We rank in differing levels of importance the things that we do, the experiences we undergo, the elements that make up our daily existence. We construct this daily existence by following a certain order, we reorganize it and order it according to a scale of values, of which we are only partially conscious; this scale is implanted in us even if we claim to have no beliefs. So the function for theater that interests me is to overturn or, even better, to erase it. My aim is to draw out a dehierarchized daily existence [*un quotidien dé-hiérarchisé*]. (*Ecrits sur le théâtre*, 134)[6]

The reflection on the role of the media, and of television in particular, is another feature of these plays that has its counterpart in much postmodernist writing. And yet, despite these similarities, the label postmodernist seems too restricting for the range and ambition of Vinaver's oeuvre. Vinaver has none of the love of pastiche that is typical of postmodernism; with the one exception of the short farce *Le Dernier sursaut,* which Vitez asked him to write as a curtain raiser to a Molière play at the Comédie Française, he never indulges in imitations, or "take-offs." Vinaver's own essays on contemporary theater suggest that he identifies postmodern theater with the theater of visual extravagance about which he is so critical. His analysis of the trap into which the "big-spending" directors have fallen (see page 138) explicitly states that these directors are spurred on to each new production not by thematic or formal concerns but, instead, by an autoreflexive fascination with the generation of images whose only aim and function is to be different from whatever has gone before: this is "the logic of difference." Patrice Pavis has defined *postmodern theater* in similar terms, identifying a "process of narcissistic self-contemplation in the postmodern work, which isolates it proudly from any influence or inheritance of contents by reducing it to the consciousness of its own homeostatic and perpetual mechanism" ("The Classical Heritage of Modern Drama," 15). Pavis is referring here to directors (specifically Bob Wilson, Klaus-Michael Gruber, and Antoine Vitez), but in any case it is clear that Vinaver's work cannot be accused of narcissism. In fact, Pavis argues that "authors such as Peter Handke, Michel Vinaver, Samuel Beckett and Heiner Müller" cannot be termed postmodern since their texts are not infinitely manipulable: "even theater of the absurd is a modernist (rather than postmodern) manifestation, since its nonsense still makes sense and recalls an interpretation and conception of the world" (7–8).

By contrast with the infinite play of difference extolled in postmodern art, Vinaver's work implies a worldview and depends on an authoritative text. Writing in 1981 about the "pathological relationship" that had developed between authors and directors in France, he challenged the then fashionable notion that the playwright's text should be seen as essentially subordinate to the visual stage image. He was not ashamed to quote D'Aubignac, who said in 1657 that *"au théâtre parler c'est agir"* (in the theater to speak is to act), and insisted on the importance of "the poetic force of the text, its 'resistance,' its density as a complete literary entity having its own existence independent of any production" ("Sur la patholo-

gie de la relation auteur metteur en scène," 132).[7] Thus, although his art
is self-conscious, always ready to challenge its own creative premises,
and although he questions both conventional notions of what art should
be and conventional "commonsense" views of reality, weaving together
and counterpointing widely discrepant levels of discourse, these qualities
take their place in a context that is Modernist rather than Postmodernist.
His restless experimentation is driven by the ambition to reach out and
touch reality in more immediate ways than are allowed by inherited dramatic structures and to reach the point where, as Beckett wrote of Proust,
form *is* content, content *is* form. If, as H. Porter Abbott has persuasively
argued (see Brater and Cohn, *Around the Absurd,* 73–96), Beckett should
be seen as a late Modernist and Beckett's ego as a Modernist one, then
Vinaver is also a late Modernist, and his is a Modernist world.

In *The Politics of Modernism,* Raymond Willams showed the links
that can be established between the concerns of modernism and the politics of Brecht. "Complex seeing" (the term he used to sum up Brecht's
art) was the product of a playwright who combined the fundamental concerns of modernism with a determination to confront contemporary reality
in all its aspects. Brecht himself once wrote that a modern theater worthy
of the name would be able to show how everything is linked—how a
decision made in a Chicago boardroom can affect the life of a peasant
living on the west coast of Ireland (*The Messingkauf Dialogues,* 23). This
is precisely the kind of complex linkage achieved in the theater of Michel
Vinaver. Vinaver's preoccupation with everyday reality and his search for
an art form in direct contact with the contemporary world resulted in a
drama of multiple viewpoints bringing its own kind of complex seeing,
different from that of Brecht but carrying the same challenge to conventional ways of considering reality, the same ironic humor and use of
distancing effects, and the same refusal to allow an artificial separation
of human experience into private and public domains. The surface texture
of his plays sparkles with irony, but underlying this is a serious engagement with reality, one that, without ever denying the strength and inhumanity of "the system," is nevertheless grounded in a fundamental Humanist optimism. In 1984 Vinaver spoke of the attitude toward reality
that characterized Erdman's work, and his words serve well to define his
own outlook: it is one combining *"clémence et ironie, tendresse et morsure"* (clemency and irony, tenderness and bite) (*Théâtre I,* 32).

NOTES

1. Le théâtre a tout à gagner à se fonder sur des textes qui lui résistent, qui font résistance notamment à l'acteur et au metteur en scène—des textes "insolubles" suivant l'expression d'Antoine Vitez—et que l'apparition de tels textes ne saurait être favorisée par la participation de l'auteur au travail du plateau.

2. Il ne s'offre pas comme un ensemble de problèmes à résoudre, mais comme une configuration de signes imposant une réalité. Son objet n'est pas de démontrer comment est fait le monde, mais de donner le monde immédiatement.

3. L'issue dialectique suggérée ici est *un langage nouveau*. Il faut entendre ce mot au sens plein, comme une découverte et une conversion de la parole, qui entraîne un nouvel *usage* du réel. [Note: *Usage* doit s'entendre ici au sens brechtien: "Ce dont j'ai besoin, c'est d'un nouveau grand usage que nous allons immédiatement instituer: l'usage qui consiste à réfléchir à neuf dans chaque situation nouvelle" *(Neinsager)*.] Une telle conversion n'exclut pas forcément la plénitude politique. On en trouverait un exemple dans la conversion de "langage" opérée récemment entre la Russie de Staline et celle de Krouchtchev, dont on voit assez dès maintenant qu'elle affecte *tout* le réel. *Mutatis mutandis, Aujourd'hui* essaye un certain langage de l'assentiment, on dirait ailleurs: de la *coexistence,* ce mot n'étant pas pris ici au sens restreint de la politique internationale, mais au sens général de: dépôt du "ressentiment," *correction* dans la reconnaisance du caractère *immédiat* du réel (*Aujourd'hui,* comme son titre l'indique, donne le présent comme une matière *immédiatement* structurable et contredit le dogme traditionnel de la Révolution comme durée essentiellement eschatalogique).

4. Ce sont des mouvement indéfinissables qui glissent très rapidement aux limites de notre conscience; ils sont à l'origine de nos gestes, de nos paroles, des sentiments que nous manifestons, que nous croyons éprouver et qu'il est impossible de définir. Ils me paraissaient et me paraissent encore constituer la source secrète de notre existence.

5. C'est la primauté du rythme par lequel il y a poussée vers le sens; c'est le traitement contrapuntique d'une multiplicité de thèmes autonomes; c'est la prééminence des thèmes sur les éléments d'intrigue; c'est le mouvement donné aux thèmes pour qu'ils s'entrechoquent ou se frottent les uns aux autres jusqu'au point de fusion plutôt qu'un enchaînement de mouvement causal; c'est l'antériorité de la parole, les personnages se constituant à partir de l'éruption du tout-venant des mots; c'est l'émergence à tâtons d'une structure partant à la découverte d'elle-même plutôt que la mise en place d'un cadre préexistant (un sujet, une situation, des personnages); c'est la niveau moléculaire où la jointure se fait entre le plus universel et le plus trivial, entre le mythique et le quotidien, entre le plus ancien et l'absolument actuel; . . . c'est la pratique de l'assemblage, du collage, du lacérage; et c'est aussi une indigence verbale, le dos tourné au beau langage, à l'ornement.

6. Constamment, sous la pression sociale, pour suivre, nous hiérarchisons. Nous dotons de niveaux différents d'importance les choses que nous faisons, les événements que nous subissons, les éléments qui entrent dans notre quotidien. Notre quotidien

nous le composons sans cesse, suivant un certain ordre, nous l'aménageons, nous l'ordonnons d'après un échelle de valeurs qui n'est consciente que pour une part; cette échelle nous habite, même si nous croyons ne croire à rien. Alors l'usage du théâtre qui m'intéresse, c'est de bousculer, mieux, d'effacer tout cela. Ce que je cherche, c'est à dégager un quotidien dé-hiérarchisé.

7. La charge poétique du texte, sa "résistance," sa densité en tant qu'objet littéraire abouti, ayant une existence indépendante de toute représentation.

Chronology

1927   Birth in Paris of Michel Grinberg. His family was of Russian Jewish origins on both sides: Léon Grinberg, his father, had left Russia in the course of the Soviet revolution at the age of twenty, when his family emigrated to France; he worked as an antique dealer, at first helping in his uncle's shop A la Vieille Russie in Paris, later setting up a second shop with the same name on Fifth Avenue in New York when the family fled there from the Nazi occupation. Léon met Sophie Vinaver in Paris, and they were married in 1925; she had also left Russia for France with her family when she was fifteen. Her father promptly set up a law practice in Paris, and his daughter followed him into the legal profession, eventually becoming head of the women's rights section of the Human Rights Department of the United Nations Organization in New York after the war. The Grinberg background was commercial, with a sensitivity and a gift for the arts. The Vinaver household was steeped in a tradition of intellectual pursuit and social commitment. Michel's maternal grandfather, Maxim Vinaver, had been a prominent lawyer working in Petersburg, a leader of the Jewish community, and involved in national politics. As a leader of the Constitutional Democratic party and a former member of the First Duma, he was forced to flee in 1919, set up his practice in Paris, and bought a house near the lake of Annecy in 1923. Michel's brother, Georges, was born in 1929.

1932–38   Primary schooling in Paris. From an early age he knew that he wanted to be a writer; at eleven he wrote his first play, *La Révolte des légumes* (see *Ecrits sur le théâtre,* fig. 36), and a piece of fiction, "Une Journée d'école." He also remembers being taken to see *Julius Caesar* directed and performed by Dullin in 1937—his first exposure to the theater.

1938   Secondary schooling began in Paris, but, with the German occupation of France in 1940, the family moved to the Zone Libre; in April 1941 they sailed to New York. The latter half of his secondary schooling was at the Lycée Français of New York, 1942–44.

1944   After passing his *baccalauréat* in June 1944 he obtained a scholarship and was admitted, as a junior, for the summer semester at Wesleyan University, Middletown, Connecticut (July–October 1944).

1944–45   National Service: a year spent in a barracks in France after he had volunteered for the Free French Forces; a frustrating period because the administrative disorder prevailing in the French army at that time barred him from participating in the final stage of the war.

1946–47   University: he returned to the United States, where, between February 1946 and February 1947, he completed his course in English and American literature at Wesleyan University. While there, he came under the influence of three teachers: Norman Brown, who taught a course on the anthropological origins of Greek drama; Fred Millett, who, when Michel became stuck on the dissertation he had planned on Kafka, suggested that he submit a collection of original short stories instead; he had already published one short story, "The Joker," in the student magazine (this was the occasion of a bizarre episode with his father, who was convinced that he had read the story somewhere before; later it was published in France as "Je trouvai ma voie"); and Newton Arvin, who introduced him to contemporary poetry, notably that of Eliot and Pound.

1946   Published his first article, "Les Américains," in *Esprit*. Michel adopted Vinaver as his pen name. When Camus came to New York on a lecture tour Vinaver succeeded in making his acquaintance and telling him of his admiration for *L'Etranger*.

1947   Awarded bachelor of arts degree with honors in English and American literature in February; he went straight to Manchester (England) to stay with his Uncle Eugène Vinaver (professor of Romance language and literature at Manchester University), where he began to translate *The Waste Land*. On his return to Paris he enrolled for a *licence libre* at the Sorbonne. On his twentieth birthday he received from his father a piece of text written out with no note of explanation to accompany it; he made this the first page of his first novel, *Lataume ou la vie quotidienne*. After reading "Le Degré zéro de l'écriture" in *Combat* (1 August 1947) he made contact with Roland Barthes and formed a friendship, which lasted until the death of Barthes (in 1980). Once his novel was finished he took it to Camus, who had encouraged him to do so when they had met in New York. Camus's response was positive, and, as a member of Gallimard's advisory committee, he recommended its publication. Vinaver immediately began work on *L'Objecteur*, inspired by an incident that had occurred during his national service: "Je me suis sans préméditation assis dans la cour et il n'a pas été possible au sergent qui commandait ce petit groupe de soldats de me faire lever; donc on m'a emporté à l'infirmerie. [I sat down without premeditation on the parade ground, and it proved impossible for the sergeant in command of the squad to get me to stand up; so they carried me to the infirmary.]"

1950   *Lataume* published; also "Le Gag de la charte" in *Les Temps Modernes*. After completing his *licence* he considered the possibility of going into teaching and worked for a while as a librarian in the Centre International de L'Enfance.

1951   *L'Objecteur* published by Gallimard. Awarded the Prix Fénéon. Vinaver described both novels as built around a central character who is completely insignificant, inspired by Eliot's J. Alfred Prufrock and by Henri Michaux's Monsieur Plume. Vinaver asked Gallimard for translation work and was offered *Loving* by Henry Green. (This later provided him with much of the material for *Iphigénie Hôtel*.)

1953   Publications: "Je trouvai ma voie" in *La Table Ronde;* "Essai sur un roman" in *Les Lettres Nouvelles* (the novel in question was *Loving*). Deciding he should not try to support himself by writing, he advertised for a job in the *International Herald Tribune* (using the wording quoted by Passemar at the beginning of *Par-dessus bord*). The advertisement was answered by Gillette, who hired him on the mistaken assumption that he had a legal background. Gillette was relocating its French offices to Annecy, so he went to live in his grandparents' house. In October he was appointed *chef de service, administration* (a small department of three or four people). Gillette decided it wanted to put Toni "home perm" kits on the French market. Grinberg was put in charge of a campaign to bring pressure on the French government to repeal an article passed in 1949 (as a result of lobbying by the national association of hairdressers) forbidding the sale of *acide thioglycolique* (an essential ingredient of the kits). A long campaign was highlighted by the publication of a treatise by Grinberg in 1956, "Une Controverse à l'ordre du jour," but, just when the law was at the point of being repealed, the British manager of Gillette Europe decided not to market the kits in France after all. This was an important formative experience for the young writer, especially concerning the intermingling of political, economic, and private motivations, as tensions build up and are released in the real world.

1954   Publication of *Amour* (translation of *Loving*) and of Vinaver's first article on theater for *Théâtre Populaire*—an account of Gabriel Monnet's first summer festival production of *Hamlet* at Annecy.

1955   Publication of "Les Mythes de la Grèce ancienne: une marche d'approche" in *Critique,* an extended review article on a translation of Hesiod by Vinaver's former professor Norman Brown. Vinaver took part in Monnet's second summer festival. Monnet suggested that Vinaver write a play; *Aujourd'hui* was finished on 2 November 1955. On a business visit to Lyon Vinaver was struck by the work of a young company headed by Roger Planchon, the Théâtre de la Comédie. He offered the company his play, which was accepted for performance the following season.

1956   Publication of *Les Coréens* by Gallimard. In the course of the third Annecy festival he met Catherine le Tellier. October: first production of *Les Coréens* at Lyon—a critical success, but right-wing demonstrators caused political disturbances outside the theater.

1957   Production of *Les Coréens* by Jean-Marie Serreau in Paris; Monnet planned performances of the play for his summer festival, to be held at Serre-Ponçon, where a vast temporary town had been erected for the workers imported from North Africa to build the hydroelectric dam, but the minister for youth and sports censored Monnet's choice of play. In its place Monnet produced Sophocles' *Antigone*, with new choral passages written by Vinaver, performed in the costumes for *Les Coréens*. Vinaver married Catherine le Tellier. He wrote his second play, *Les Huissiers*.

1958   Publication of *Les Huissiers* in *Théâtre Populaire*. Adapted *The Shoe-maker's Holiday* on commission for Jean Vilar. Attended the Actor's Studio while on a business visit to New York and wrote an account of their work for *Théâtre Populaire*, which included a comparative assessment of Brecht and Stanislavsky. Spent some time in England on a sales training program.

1959   Production of *Les Coréens* by Charles Joris in Switzerland, with a company soon to become the Théâtre Populaire Romand. Vinaver experienced difficulties over Georges Wilson's production of *La Fête du cordonnier* at the Chaillot T.N.P. in March and published two articles explaining his approach to the play. Wrote *Iphigénie Hôtel* and reviewed *La Seconde surprise de l'amour*, directed by Planchon for *Théâtre Populaire*. Sent by Gillette to a nine-month management course at the IMEDE international business school in Switzerland. Birth of his first daughter, Delphine.

1960   Production of *Les Coréens* by Monnet at the Comédie de Saint-Etienne. Publication of *Iphigénie Hôtel* in *Théâtre Populaire* (version intégrale). Appointed managing director of Gillette, Belgium, where he stayed until 1964. A smallish operation (roughly forty people, which included eight or nine sales staff). Grinberg accompanied the sales staff on their rounds, observed how archaic their methods were, wrote a small salesman's manual, and ran a training program for them. His efforts met with success: the company's sales grew substantially. Birth of his second daughter, Barbara.

1961   Birth of his son, Ivan.

1963   Wrote an article for *Théâtre Populaire* on the student drama festival at Erlangen in which, for the first time, he used the phrase "par-dessus bord" (overboard). Publication: *Iphigénie Hôtel* (version scénique), Gallimard. Birth of his third daughter, Anouk, who was to enter the acting profession.

1964   Published a long article, also for *Théâtre Populaire*, reviewing Planchon's production of *Troilus and Cressida*—a focusing of his own dramaturgical preoccupations. Gillette management proposed a posting to the Middle East; he refused. Following a boardroom change, he was offered a posting to Italy and accepted. The Milan establishment consisted of about 450 employees. Gillette was moving to a policy of "creative marketing," a period of expansion and intense promotional activity.

1966   Recalled to the post of managing director in France (roughly one thousand employees) because of the unexpected departure of the previous post holder (an American whose wife refused to stay in a country where the milk was not delivered). Settled once again in Annecy.

1967 Overcame his seven-year playwright's block and began work on what was to be *Par-dessus bord*.

1968 Gillette was one of the few factories with no work stoppage during the "events" of May and June: it was highly automated, with workers among the highest paid in the region.

1969 Initiated negotiations for Gillette to acquire a controlling interest in S. T. Dupont, an old family firm near Annecy manufacturing luxury goods. Finished writing *Par-dessus bord:* running to more than 250 pages, with a cast of thirty-one named characters plus extras, it threatened to be unstageable, but at least Vinaver counted on publication.

1970 *Par-dessus bord* turned down for publication by Jacques Lemarchand, drama editor at Gallimard. S. T. Dupont purchased by Gillette, who put Grinberg in as managing director (a post he retained until 1978).

1971 *Par-dessus bord* accepted for publication by Robert Voisin, director of L'Arche and Brecht enthusiast. Vinaver wrote *La Demande d'emploi,* a small-scale work with a cast of four.

1972 Publication of *Par-dessus bord*. Staged reading of *La Demande d'emploi* by Jean-Pierre Dougnac in the Théâtre Ouvert series at the Avignon festival. Vinaver became involved with a young, politically active theater group in Annecy, the Théâtre Eclaté, providing support when their funding was threatened following their production of an outspoken political play, *La Farce de Burgos*.

1973 Publication of *La Demande d'emploi* by L'Arche. Production of *Par-dessus bord,* cut, remodeled, and directed by Planchon; performed at Villeurbanne and at Paris. Production of *La Demande d'emploi* by Dougnac in Paris. Another production by André Steiger in Switzerland the same year was followed by several others in subsequent years.

1976 Wrote two more short chamber plays: *Dissident, il va sans dire* and *Nina, c'est autre chose*. The S. T. Dupont factory at Faverges went on a prolonged strike, with flashes of violence and workers occupying the building.

1977 Production of *Iphigénie Hôtel* (eighteen years after it was written) by Antoine Vitez with the company of his Théâtre des Quartiers d'Ivry, at the Centre Georges Pompidou, Paris: a critical success. Wrote *Les Travaux et les jours* inspired, to a degree, by the strike and occupation of the previous year.

1978 Publication of *Dissident* and *Nina* as *Théâtre de chambre* by L'Arche and production of the two in a double bill at the studio theater of the Théâtre de L'Est Parisien by Jacques Lassalle—the start of a long and fruitful association between author and director. This production enjoyed critical success and was awarded the Syndicat de la Critique's prize for the best new French play. Many other productions of these plays have followed. Grinberg resigned from the management of S. T. Dupont but retained an advisory post at Gillette.

1979   Wrote *A la Renverse*, a play with televised sequences. Publication of *Les Travaux et les jours;* Alain Françon, director of the Théâtre Eclaté of Annecy, mounted a staged reading of the play and laid plans for a full production. Grinberg separated from Gillette.

1980   Production of *Les Travaux et les jours* by Alain Françon and the Théâtre Eclaté performed at Annecy and Paris—again a critical success; Vinaver had the paradoxical experience of being hailed a promising new writer in his fifties. Production of *Les Huissiers* (twenty-three years after it was written) by Gilles Chavassieux at his theater Les Ateliers (Lyon). Wrote an adaptation of Nicolai Erdman's *The Suicide,* working from a literal translation from the Russian he made with his father. Publication of a children's book, *Les Histoires de Rosalie,* based on stories of his maternal grandmother's childhood in late nineteenth-century Russia. Publication of *A la Renverse* by L'Aire and production at the Chaillot National Theater (formerly T.N.P.) by Lassalle. This time the press were hostile; only the television sequences were praised.

1981   Wrote *L'Ordinaire,* sparked off by the story of a plane crash in the Andes several years before, which the passengers survived by eating the flesh of the dead. Publication of *Le Livre des Huissiers,* edited by Vinaver and Michelle Henry, by Limage–Alin Avila: the text of the play supplemented by a collage of contemporary photographs and news items.

1982   Commissioned by the Comédie Française to write an adaptation of Gorki's *Summerfolk,* to be directed by Lassalle. Began teaching at the University of Paris III (Censier). Publication by L'Aire of his collected writings on the theater, *Ecrits sur le théâtre,* edited by Michelle Henry. Appointed to chair the newly established drama committee of the Centre National des Lettres, where he began an inquiry into the crisis of theater publishing in France.

1983   Publication of *L'Ordinaire* by L'Aire; this was the occasion for Vinaver's first (and last) venture in stage directing: in collaboration with Françon he directed the play at the Gémier Theatre (studio) at Chaillot. Mixed critical response, but the stature of the play was generally recognized. The first complete production of *Par-dessus bord* given by the Théâtre Populaire Romand (Switzerland), directed by Joris, to inaugurate their new theater. Production of *Les Estivants* at the Comédie Française directed by Lassalle.

1984   Production of *Le Suicidé* by the Comédie Française at the Odéon, directed by Jean-Pierre Vincent. Wrote *Les Voisins* and *Portrait d'une femme.* Began a play-writing workshop at the University of Paris III.

1986   Production of *Les Voisins* by Françon at Théâtre Ouvert in Paris and on tour at a number of centres dramatiques—Vinaver's greatest success with the critics. Publication of *Théâtre I* and *Théâtre II* by Actes Sud in association with L'Aire. Awarded Ibsen prize. At the Avignon festival presented the findings of his inquiry for the Centre National des Lettres, published the following year as "Le Compte rendu d'Avignon." Wrote *Mémoire sur mes travaux,* on the basis of which he was granted recognized teacher status in the university. Publication of *Chamber Theater* in American translation by Paul Antal, by P.A.J. Books.

1987   Publication of *Le Compte rendu d'Avignon* by Actes Sud; its broad-ranging review of the current state of the playwright in the French theater was widely praised, and most of its recommendations adopted. First production of his work in Britain: *Les Travaux et les jours*, translated by Peter Meyer as *A Smile on the End of the Line*, directed by Sam Walters at the Orange Tree Theater, Richmond.

1988   Wrote *L'Emission de télévision*. Appointed titular professor in the Drama Department at the University of Paris VIII (Saint-Denis), where he continues to teach text analysis and creative writing.

1989   Publication of *L'Emission de télévision* by Actes Sud and of *Portrait of a Woman*, English translation by Donald Watson, by Methuen. Production of *La Demande d'emploi*, translated by John Burgess as *Situation Vacant*, directed by Walters at the Orange Tree. A second British production of *Les Travaux et les jours*, translated by Ron Butlin as *Blending In*, was staged at the Traverse Theater for the Edinburgh Festival. Vinaver was commissioned by Vitez to write an impromptu for the yearly Molière celebration at the Comédie Française; the result was a short pastiche farce: *Le Dernier sursaut*. Production of *Les Voisins* by Joris at the Théâtre Populaire Romand. Commissioned by the Comédie de Genève to write an adaptation of *Julius Caesar*.

1990   Production of *L'Emission de télévision* by the Comédie Française at the Odéon, directed by Lassalle. Mixed critical response. Special festival of readings from Vinaver's work organized by Théâtre Ouvert under the title "Itinéraire de Michel Vinaver." Staged reading of *Portrait of a Woman*, directed by Di Trevis for the Royal Shakespeare Company at the first Covent Garden International Festival. Publication of *Le Dernier sursaut* and of *Jules César* by Actes Sud. Production of *Jules César*, directed by Claude Stratz, at the Comédie de Genève.

1991   Publication in *New Theatre Quarterly* of "Decentralization as Chiaroscuro," the text of a paper given by Vinaver the previous year when he was invited as keynote speaker to the First Birmingham University Regional Playwrights' Conference. Production of *Le Temps et la chambre*, a translation of *Die Zeit und das zimmer* by Botho Strauss, commissioned and directed by Patrice Chéreau at the Odéon; publication by L'Arche.

Bibliography

Works by Vinaver

Published Books

1950 *Lataume*. Paris: Gallimard.
1951 *L'Objecteur*. Paris: Gallimard.
1956 *Les Coréens*. Paris: Gallimard.
1963 *Iphigénie Hôtel* (version scénique). Paris: Gallimard.
1972 *Par-dessus bord*. Paris: L'Arche.
1973 *La Demande d'emploi*. Paris: L'Arche.
1978 *Théâtre de chambre*. Paris: L'Arche.
1979 *Les Travaux et les jours*. Paris: L'Arche.
1980 *A la Renverse*. Lausanne: L'Aire.
       Les Histoires de Rosalie. Paris: Castor Poche Flammarion.
1981 *Le Livre des Huissiers*. Paris: Limage–Alin Avila.
1982 *Ecrits sur le théâtre*. Lausanne: L'Aire.
       Lapiaz: anatomie d'un paysage (photographs by Michel Séméniako and words by Michel Vinaver). Paris: Passage.
1983 *L'Ordinaire*. Lausanne: L'Aire.
       Par-dessus bord (collection du répertoire). La Chaux-de-Fonds: Théâtre Populaire Romand.
1985 *Les Français vus par les français* (by Guy Nevers, alias Michel Vinaver). Paris: Barrault.
1986 *Théâtre complet* (2 vols.). Arles: Actes Sud; Lausanne: L'Aire.
1987 *Le Compte rendu d'Avignon*. Arles: Actes Sud.
1989 *Les Voisins* (collection du répertoire). La Chaux-de-Fonds: Théâtre Populaire Romand.
       L'Emission de télévision. Arles: Actes Sud.
1990 *Le Dernier sursaut*. Arles: Actes Sud.

Unpublished Dissertation

1986 "Mémoire sur mes travaux." Presented to the University of Paris.

Individual Plays

Les Coréens. Gallimard, 1956. Also in *Théâtre I,* 1986.
Les Huissiers, in *Théâtre Populaire,* 29 March 1958. Also in *Le Livre des Huissiers.*
Paris: Limage–Alin Avila, 1981; and in *Théâtre I,* 1986.
Iphigénie Hôtel, in *Théâtre Populaire* 39, 3e. trim (1960). Shortened stage version:
Gallimard, 1963; another, shortened version made in collaboration with Antoine
Vitez, in *Théâtre I,* 1986.
Par dessus-bord. L'Arche, 1972; reprint, Théâtre Populaire Romand, 1983. Also in
Acteurs (August–September and October 1987); another shortened version in
Théâtre I, 1986.
La Demande d'emploi. L'Arche, 1973. Also in *Théâtre I,* 1986.
Dissident, il va sans dire and *Nina, c'est autre chose,* in *Théâtre de chambre.*
L'Arche, 1978. Also in *Théâtre II,* 1986.
Les Travaux et les jours. L'Arche, 1979. Also in *Théâtre II,* 1986.
A la Renverse. L'Aire, 1980. Also in *Théâtre II,* 1986.
L'Ordinaire. L'Aire, 1983. Also in *Théâtre II,* 1986.
Les Voisins, in *Théâtre II,* 1986. Also in *L'Avant-Scène* (November 1986).
Portrait d'une femme, in *Théâtre II,* 1986.
L'Emission de télévision. Arles: Actes Sud, 1989.
Le Dernier sursaut. Arles: Actes Sud, 1990.

Translations and Adaptations

Amour (trans. of Henry Green's novel *Loving*). Paris: Gallimard, 1954.
La Fête du cordonnier (from Thomas Dekker's play *The Shoemaker's Holiday*). Paris:
Théâtre National Populaire (collection du répertoire), 1959. Also in *Théâtre I,* 1986.
Les Estivants (from Maksim Gorky's play *Summerfolk*). Paris: Comédie Française
(collection du répertoire), 1983. Also in *Théâtre II,* 1986.
Le Suicidé (from Nicolai Erdman's play *The Suicide*), in *L'Avant-Scène* (1984). Also
in *Théâtre II,* 1986.
La Terre vague (trans. of T. S. Eliot's poem *The Waste Land*), in *Poésie* 31 (1984).
Jules César (trans. of Shakespeare's *Julius Caesar*). Arles: Actes Sud, 1990.
Le Temps et la chambre (trans. of Botho Strauss's play *Die Zeit und das zimmer*).
Paris: L'Arche, 1991.

Productions

A chronology of productions, drawn up by Michel Vinaver and listing actors, producers, etc., is included as an appendix to *Vinaver dramaturge* by Anne Ubersfeld (Paris: Librairie Théâtrale, 1989).

Selected Articles

Vinaver's writings on his own plays from *Les Coréens* to *A la Renverse* are collected in *Ecrits sur le théâtre,* together with a great many other short pieces, some of which had been published before, some not. The following list includes only the most important of his articles; where these have been reprinted in *Ecrits sur le théâtre*, the page reference is indicated.

1946 "Les Américains," *Esprit* (November).

1950 "Le Gag de la charte," *Les Temps Modernes* 62 (December).

1953 "Je trouvai ma voie" (short story), *La Table Ronde* 65 (May).

"Essai sur un roman," *Les Lettres Nouvelles* 4 and 5 (June and July).

1954 *"Hamlet* à Annecy," *Théâtre Populaire* 9 (September); also in *Ecrits sur le théâtre*, 23–27.

1955 "Les Mythes de la Grèce ancienne: une marche d'approche," *Critique* 94 and 95 (March and April).

"Une Expérience radicale: *Ubu Roi* aux Nuits Théâtrales d'Annecy," *Ecrits sur le théâtre*, 31–35.

1958 "La Fin et les moyens de l'acteur, 1: Actor's Studio; 2: Stanislavski et Brecht," *Théâtre Populaire* 32, 4e. trim; also in *Ecrits sur le théâtre*, 50–76.

1959 *"La Seconde surprise de l'amour," Théâtre Populaire* 34, 2e. trim; also in *Ecrits sur le théâtre*, 77–80.

"De l'adaptation," *Bref* (March); also in *Ecrits sur le théâtre*, 80–85.

"Théâtre et sécurité," *Les Lettres Françaises* (19 March); also in *Ecrits sur le théâtre*, 85–88.

1963 "Le Festival d'Erlangen," *Théâtre Populaire* 51, 3e. trim; also in *Ecrits sur le théâtre*, 89–93.

1964 "Itinéraire de Roger Planchon," *Théâtre Populaire* 54, 2e. trim; also in *Ecrits sur le théâtre*, 94–108.

1973 "L'Ecriture enchevêtrée et l'indifférencié due langage—entretien avec Emile Copfermann," *Travail Théâtral* 12 (July–September); also in *Ecrits sur le théâtre*, 274–83.

1975 "Marx, les fruits et la spéculation: a propos de *Par-dessus bord*—entretien avec Roger Planchon et Michel Vinaver," *La Nouvelle Critique* 85 (July): 34–37.

1976 "Le Sens et le plaisir d'écrire—entretien avec Jean-Pierre Sarrazac," *Travail Théâtral* 24–25 (July–December); also in *Ecrits sur le théâtre*, 284–90.

1978 "Un Comique de découverte—entretien avec Dominique Chautemps," *ATAC Informations* 91 (February): 50–56; also in *Ecrits sur le théâtre*, 291–301.

"Auto-interrogatoire," *Travail Théâtral* 30 (January–March): 47–57; also in *Ecrits sur le théâtre*, 303–17.

1979 "Le Théâtre et le quotidien," in *Les Travaux et les jours*. Paris: L'Arche, 1979; also in *Ecrits sur le théâtre*, 123–26.

1980 "La Banalité dans le désordre—entretien avec Jean-Pierre Léonardini," *ATAC Informations* 112 (November): 6–8.

1981 "Boris de Schloezer, Eléments d'un portrait," in *Boris de Schloezer*. Paris: Centre Pompidou and Pandora.

"Une Ecriture du quotidien," *Théâtre Public* 39 (May–June); also in *Ecrits sur le théâtre*, 126–34.

1982 "Sur la pathologie de la relation auteur metteur en scène," in *L'Annuel du Théâtre 1981–1982*, 131–33. Lausanne: L'Aire.

1983   "Théâtre pour l'oeil, théâtre pour l'oreille," in *L'Annuel du Théâtre 1982– 1983*, 138–39. Lausanne: L'Aire.
1984   "Le Théâtre entre deux chaises: objet de spectacle, objet de lecture" and "Sur la condition de l'auteur dramatique en France aujourd'hui," in *Auteurs dramatiques français d'aujourd'hui*, 182–88 and 219–20. Amiens: Maison de la Culture.
1985   "Sur Attoun," *Théâtre en Europe* 8 (October): 130–31.
1987   "Six heures en compagnie de Michel Vinaver" (video). Paris and Annecy: Production FALS'DOC (Paris) and Centre d'Action Culturel of Annecy (a fifty-minute version is also available on videocassette).
        "Comment Kokkos travaille," *Théâtre en Europe* 13 (April): 76.
        "Questions de Théâtre," *Poésie* 41 (June): 56–59.
        "Un géant parmi les oncles," *Théâtre en Europe* 15 (October): 18–26 (discussion on Ibsen between Vinaver and Peter Zadek).
1988   "La Mise en trop," *Théâtre Public* 82–83 (July–October): 82–83.
        "L'Ile," *Théâtre en Europe* 18 (September): 21–22.
1989   "Ici et Maintenant," *L'Art du Théâtre* (10): 39–42.
        "Entretien entre Michel Vinaver et Jean-Loup Rivière," in *Les Voisins*, 7–78. La Chaux-de-Fonds: Théâtre Populaire Romand (interviews first broadcast on France-Culture in the series "A voix nue," 29 February to 4 March 1988).
1990   "Le Texte doit rester un objet insoluble—entretien avec Olivier Ortolani." Program for *L'Emission de télévision* at the Théâtre National de Strasbourg, 7–15.
1991   "Decentralization as Chiaroscuro," *New Theatre Quarterly* 25 (February): 64–76.
        "L'Apprenti auteur dramatique" (with Mike Sens), *Théâtre/Public* 99:36–43.

Plays Translated into English

1986   *Chamber Theater: Dissident, Goes without Saying* and *Nina, It's Different*, in *Drama in Contemporary France*, ed. Philippa Wehle; trans. Paul Antal. New York: P.A.J.
1988   *The Neighbors*, in *The Paris Stage*, trans. Paul Antal. New York: Ubu Repertory Theater.
1989   *Portrait of a Woman*, in *New French Plays*, ed. David Bradby and Claude Schumacher; trans. Donald Watson. London: Methuen.

There are several other unpublished translations of Vinaver's plays, which may be obtained by applying to his British agent, Michael Imison, 28 Almeida Street, London N1 1TD.

Secondary Sources

Adamov, Arthur. 1964. *Ici et maintenant*. Paris: Gallimard.
———. 1970. "Presque—le théâtre et le rêve," *Les Lettres Françaises* (4 February).
Barthes, Roland. 1953. *Le Degré zéro de l'ecriture*. Paris: Seuil.

———. 1957. *Mythologies*. Paris: Seuil.

———. 1964. *Essais critiques*. Paris: Seuil.

———. 1978. "Note sur *Aujourd'hui*," *Travail Théâtral* 30:58–60.

Borges, Jorge Luis. 1970. *Labyrinths*. Harmondsworth: Penguin.

Bradby, David. 1984. *The Theatre of Roger Planchon*. Cambridge: Chadwyck-Healey.

———. 1988. "'Entre le Mythique et le Quotidien': Myth in the Theatre of Michel Vinaver," in *Myth and Its Making in the French Theatre*, 205–14. Cambridge: Cambridge University Press.

———. 1991. *Modern French Drama, 1940–1990*, 2d ed. Cambridge: Cambridge University Press.

Bradby, David, and David Williams. 1988. *Directors' Theatre*. London: Macmillan.

Brater, Enoch, and Ruby Cohn, eds. 1990. *Around the Absurd*. Ann Arbor: University of Michigan Press.

Brecht, Bertolt. 1964. *Brecht on Theatre*, ed. and trans. John Willett. London: Methuen.

———. 1965. *The Messingkauf Dialogues*, trans. John Willett. London: Methuen.

———. 1977. "He Who Says No," in *The Measures Taken and Other Lehrstücke*, London: Methuen.

Camus, Albert. 1962. *Théâtre, récits, nouvelles*. Paris: Gallimard.

———. 1964. *Carnets: Janvier 1942–Mars 1951*. Paris: Gallimard.

Corvin, Michel, ed. 1991. *Dictionnaire Encyclopédique du Théâtre*. Paris: Bordas.

Daoust, Yvette. 1981. *Roger Planchon*. Cambridge: Cambridge University Press.

Dort, Bernard. 1960. *Lecture de Brecht*. Paris: Seuil.

———. 1967. *Théâtre Public*. Paris: Seuil.

———. 1971. *Théâtre réel*. Paris: Seuil.

———. 1979. *Le Théâtre en jeu*. Paris: Seuil.

———. 1988. *La Représentation emancipée*. Arles: Actes Sud.

Eagleton, Terry. 1991. *Ideology: An Introduction*. London: Verso.

Eliot, T. S. 1963. *Collected Poems, 1909–1962*. London: Faber and Faber.

Ertel, Evelyne. 1991. "Itinéraire de Michel Vinaver," *Théâtre Public* 97:36–40.

Flaubert, Gustave. 1952. *Dictionnaire des Idées reçues*, in *Oeuvres II*, 999–1023. Paris: Gallimard.

Gatti, Armand. 1964. *Chant public devant deux chaises électriques*. Paris: Seuil.

Hutcheon, Linda. 1988. *A Poetics of Postmodernism*. London: Routledge.

———. 1989. *The Politics of Postmodernism*. London: Routledge.

Jomaron, Jacqueline, ed. 1988. *Le Théâtre en France*. Vol. 1. Paris: Colin.

———. 1989. *Le Théâtre en France*. Vol. 2. Paris: Colin.

Jones, David. 1937. *In Parenthesis*. London: Faber and Faber.

Joris, Charles. 1983. "Une Comédie des pouvoirs," in *Par-dessus bord*, 13–32. La Chaux-de-Fonds: Théâtre Populaire Romand.

Joyce, James. 1969. *Ulysses*. Harmondsworth: Penguin.

Kokkos, Yannis. 1978. "Théâtre de chambre: notes et relevés," *Travail Théâtral* 30:77–80.

Lassalle, Jacques. 1990. "Fable" (dramaturgical résumé of *L'Emission de télévision*). Program for Théâtre National de Strasbourg, 23–27.

Lawrence, D. H. 1971. "Sun," in *The Princess and Other Stories*. Harmondsworth: Penguin.

Lebrun, Françoise. 1978. *"Dissident, il va sans dire:* journal des répétitions," *Travail Théâtral* 30:71–76.

Pavis, Patrice. 1986. "The Classical Heritage of Modern Drama," *Modern Drama* 29, No. 1: 1–22.

Rivière, Jean-Loup. 1986. Preface to *Théâtre Complet,* by Michel Vinaver, 7–21. Arles: Actes Sud; Lausanne: L'Aire.

Sarraute, Nathalie. 1939. *Tropismes*. Paris: Denoel.

———. 1956. *L'Ere du soupçon*. Paris: Gallimard.

———. 1964. *L'Ere du soupçon*. Paris: Gallimard ("idées").

Sarrazac, Jean-Pierre. 1975. "L'Ecriture au présent," *Travail Théâtral* 18–19:55–85.

———. 1976. "L'Ecriture au présent," *Travail Théâtral* 24–25:88–102.

———. 1978. "La Pléthore et la rareté: le montage dans *Par-dessus bord,"* *Travail Théâtral* 30:61–63.

———. 1978. "Vers un Théâtre Minimal," in *Théâtre de Chambre* by Michel Vinaver, 69–77. Paris: L'Arche.

———. 1981. *L'Avenir du drame*. Lausanne: L'Aire.

———. 1983. "Travail à la table sur *L'Ordinaire,"* in *L'Annuel du Théâtre 1982– 1983,* 181–91. Lausanne: L'Aire.

Schaetti, Bernard. 1992. "Une fable sur le temps: *Par-dessus bord,"* *Théâtre/Public* 105:50–53.

Sens, Mike. 1991. "L'Apprenti auteur dramatique" (with Michel Vinaver), *Théâtre/ Public* 99:36–43.

Simon, Yoland. 1987. *Le Système des oppositions et le jeu des conflits dans "La Demande d'emploi" de Michel Vinaver*. Le Havre: I.U.T.

States, Bert O. 1985. *Great Reckonings in Little Rooms*. Berkeley and Los Angeles: University of California Press.

Suther, Judith D. 1972. "The Medium Is Not the Message: Myth in Vinaver's *Iphigénie Hôtel,"* *French Review* 45, no. 6: 1106–16.

Szondi, Peter. 1987. *Theory of the Modern Drama,* ed. and trans. Michael Hays. Cambridge: Polity Press.

Ubersfeld, Anne. 1989. *Vinaver dramaturge*. Paris: Librairie Théâtrale. (A chronology of productions, drawn up by Michel Vinaver and listing actors, producers, etc., is included in this volume, pp. 211–23.)

———. 1992. "Vinaver au Portugal," *Théâtre/Public* 105:47–50.

Vinaver, Eugène. "Medieval Poetry and the Moderns." Unpublished lecture.

Williams, Raymond. 1968. *Drama from Ibsen to Brecht*. London: Chatto and Windus.

———. 1972. *Drama in Performance*. Harmondsworth: Penguin.

———. 1981. *Culture*. Glasgow: Fontana.

———. 1989. *The Politics of Modernism,* ed. Tony Pinkney. London: Verso.

Index